1962

Pirandello and the French Theater

*New York University Studies
in Romance Languages and Literature*

3

PIRANDELLO
and the French Theater

THOMAS BISHOP

NEW YORK UNIVERSITY PRESS · 1960

TO MURIEL

Acknowledgments

For their valuable aid, encouragement, and criticism, I should like to express my sincere gratitude to Warren Ramsey, Germaine Brée, Clarence D. Brenner, Alvin Eustis, and Giovanni Cecchetti.

I am also thankful to the several French playwrights who were good enough to correspond with me about the relation of their works to Pirandello.

Lastly, I wish to thank the Pirandello Society of America, Inc., and its President, George Freedley, for endorsing this work.

Foreword

"As IMPORTANT as the first Pirandello produced by Pitoëff in Paris in 1923," wrote Jean Anouilh of Beckett's *Waiting for Godot*. For Beckett this was high praise. But, Beckett aside, Anouilh's remark shows clearly that the first performance of Pirandello in Paris still stands out as one of the significant dates in the annals of the contemporary French stage—the most significant in Anouilh's eyes. *How* significant, Mr. Bishop demonstrates by tracing the influence of Pirandello on many French playwrights of our time, major or minor.

The intellectual mood of Paris, in the twenties, was unusually propitious to Pirandellian themes. Proust "in search of time lost," had endlessly probed the multiple, complex, and fleeting world of the self and the strange games that illusion and reality play in individual behavior. A public sympathetic to Dostoevski, at home in the Gidian world of counterfeit and with the mutations of personality characteristic of the Gidian hero was well-prepared to grasp the peculiar quality of Pirandellian characters and their elusive relation to objective facts. The twenties, after all, were the years when Freud made his way among the somewhat recalcitrant French, when the surrealists denounced the deceptive assumptions of common sense in favor of the subjective and shifting realities grasped in madness, dream, or hallucination. Breton's *Nadja* would not be out of place on a Pirandellian stage. In the early twenties, too, the serious young *Nouvelle Revue Française* ran a whole series of rather worried articles on the *mal du siècle,* diagnosed as a crisis in the concept of the self as personality. Pirandello could be sure of an audience.

The theater too—at least the avant-garde theater—was in the hands of a small group of imaginative, talented, and dedicated producers, alert to all new possibilities in the drama, from whatever direction they came. Not all playwrights, however good, find a Dullin or a Pitoëff along their path. New interpretations of Shakespeare, Molière, and Marivaux—to whom Pirandello is probably indebted—had prepared the public for plays more demanding, more sophisticated, too, than the run-of-the-mill after-dinner play of consumption. And a whole theory of the stage, born of such men as Craig and Stanislavsky among others, had accustomed the drama-minded to think in terms of a "stage-reality," a "stage-world," "stage-characters" or "personae" in their complex relation to the characters and reality encountered in life itself.

Pirandello's theater synthesized and made dramatic capital out of these many latent or explicit trends, translating them into concrete stage situations which required of his audience a certain intellectual alertness. His theater no longer made any pretense to "imitate" "real" and often insignificant situations. It transposed and, like all modern art, translated into aesthetic—not moral—terms a certain new consciousness concerning the relation of human beings to life—a rather limited consciousness no doubt, but nonetheless valid and well-integrated with his dramatic techniques.

It is fairly easy to see therefore *why* Pirandello's plays had an impact on French playwrights. It is harder to distinguish *how* his influence shaped in part their dramatic techniques or points of view. Besides Pirandello, many other influences were at

work in a theater avid for new and valid plays, reawakened too
to certain new values in the classics.

Mr. Bishop has approached his topic with clarity and com-
petence. He makes no excessive claims for Pirandello. His
analysis is direct, his conclusions straightforward and measured. His knowledge both of the French theater with which
he deals and of Pirandello is broad and sound. It is a pleasure
to read a book which scrupulously avoids pretentious theoriz-
ing and an abstruse terminology. *Pirandello and the French
Theater* is valuable both as a reference work and because of
the light it throws on one important aspect of the French
stage in the "entre-deux-guerres" period.

GERMAINE BRÉE

Contents

Introduction

LUIGI PIRANDELLO is one of the truly great names of the modern theater. His plays have been and are still being performed in many countries and in many languages, and they have been widely acclaimed both by the public and by the critics. Such universal appreciation is rare for any playwright. It is even rarer for an innovator whose works must be considered "difficult." This adjective is appropriate because the subject matter of most of Pirandello's plays lies in the realm of ideas—complex ideas concerning reality and illusion, the fluidity of the human personality, and the basic problem of artistic creation. Although the author is not a philosopher in the commonly accepted sense of that word, his theater might best be termed philosophic. His innovations were twofold: his plays brought new ideas to the stage and he increased the dimensions of the stage itself, skillfully interweaving the artificial level of the theater with the reality of life.

When Pirandello's plays were first presented in France in the early 1920's, they created a sensation unmatched by any other foreign author and unequaled by anyone in France during that period. Speaking generally, the French theater up to that time lacked great imagination, and if it had passed the stage of naturalism, it had not yet found a clearly defined new direction. Pirandello was to help give it that direction.

Since the days of the Théâtre Libre, France had been very receptive to foreign dramatists. It is not, therefore, especially surprising that an Italian author made such an impression there. What is unusual is the far-reaching effect of that impression. From the time of the initial performances of Pirandello in France to the present, many French playwrights have been influenced to some degree by the Italian author, and similarities between his dramaturgy and that of others point to a general area of agreement of ideas.

To demonstrate this contention, this book discusses the sizable number of Pirandello plays performed and revived in Paris and their favorable critical reception. Next, Pirandello's theater is analyzed in order to isolate its salient themes, which are then traced in the plays of the French writers under discussion. This procedure shows how Pirandellian ideas and techniques were introduced in France and then assimilated by a considerable segment of its major and minor dramatists, and it leads to the conclusion that the similarities between Pirandello and the modern French theater are among the most important in the annals of comparative theater.

Of course, one must be careful in using the term "influence." It is all too simple to abuse it by seeing influence everywhere only because one is looking for it everywhere. In the writing of this book, a conscious effort has been made to avoid that pitfall. On the other hand, a critic need not be excessively timid; one need not, for example, insist on a corroborating statement by an author before hazarding an opinion that he was influenced by someone else. Some authors would not want to acknowledge any influence—although the word has no derogatory connotation. Many others are unable to discuss the matter at all because they lack the perspective necessary for such an analysis. It is, after all, the critic's function, and not the author's, to study influences. In certain cases, it is more accurate to speak of an accord of ideas between two authors rather than an influence wielded by one over the other.

French playwrights were influenced by Pirandello both directly and indirectly. There were, first, those who found the essence of Pirandellism in the Italian's theater itself—on stage or in printed versions. The indirect influence is more delicate, based on the Pirandellian elements in the works of those who had absorbed them directly. Pirandellism became a part of the French theater through the great number of French plays which reflect it and because the Italian's plays, performed almost constantly in Paris for thirty-five years, are now familiar fixtures in the Parisian theater.

Many of the playwrights treated in this work have expressed their indebtedness to Pirandello. Responsible critics have pointed to many other similar debts. In all cases, this book will attempt to demonstrate the influence or similarity by a careful thematic analysis and a study of techniques.

In books and articles commenting on the contemporary French theater, critics frequently speak of Pirandello's influence. Various studies of individual playwrights mention the Italian writer. However, no one has yet attempted a systematic examination of all the aspects of Pirandello's role in the French theater. It is hoped that this work will fill that lacuna and will demonstrate the great part that he has played.

Pirandello and the French Theater

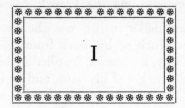

I

The Success of Pirandello

ALTHOUGH Pirandello, during his lifetime, enjoyed world-wide fame and recognition, it was not until rather late that he was so rewarded. The 1934 Nobel Prize for Literature, awarded to him at the age of sixty-seven, was the well-deserved tribute of an admiring world. It seems appropriate to begin with a brief biographical glance at his earlier years.[1]

Luigi Pirandello was born in Grigenti, Sicily, in 1867, the son of a well-to-do mine owner. His Sicilian primary and secondary education developed in him a predilection for studies, causing him to forsake the business career his parents had envisaged for him and attend the University of Rome. Following a quarrel with his professors, Pirandello moved on to Bonn, where he received his doctorate, with a dissertation, written in German, on the dialect of his native Grigenti region. On his return to Italy at the age of twenty-three, he indulged briefly in journalism and in business, but he soon turned to writing short stories and, in 1897, also accepted a position as Professor of Italian Literature at the Roman Normal College for

Women. His first major success was the novel *Il fu Mattia Pascal*, in 1904. Much of his work from this period reflects his interest in Sicily, an interest instilled in him by Giovanni Verga, then at the height of his fame, and by his friend, Luigi Capuana.

When he returned from Bonn, Pirandello and the girl to whom he was engaged broke their betrothal. His father promptly arranged a marriage for him with a young woman whom his son had never seen, and soon afterward Luigi Pirandello married Antonietta Portulano, the daughter of the senior Pirandello's business associate. In the first few years of their union, she presented him with two sons and a daughter, but tragedy soon struck the household. A mining disaster bankrupted the families of both husband and wife, and Luigi was forced to rely solely on the income from his professorship—a position which he grew to detest—until success enabled him to abandon it in 1921. However, this reversal had consequences far greater than the financial ones.

Weakened by the aftereffects of her youngest child's birth, Signora Pirandello's nerves shattered, and she lapsed into insanity. She died in an asylum in 1918, but for most of the fourteen years of her illness she lived with her husband, persecuting him with terrible fits of jealousy, making his life exceedingly bitter. Pirandello suffered silently and stoically. To appease his wife's delusions about his supposed infidelities, Pirandello remained at home during his leisure time; yet, unbearable as she caused his life to be, he refused for many years to commit her to an institution.

It is probable that in this sad experience lies an important source of the pessimism in his writings. The most pathetic of his characters suffered no more than Pirandello himself. Signora Pirandello's fantasies of Luigi's nonexistent extramarital affairs, the personality she attributed to him—a personality so different from his real one—are akin to the basic ideas in his plays.

Although he had previously dramatized some of his stories, it was not until 1916 that Pirandello turned seriously to the theater, with *Pensaci, Giacomino!* and *Liolà*. The following year he produced four plays, including two of his best known, *Così è (se vi pare)* and *Il Piacere dell'onestà*. His imagination was so fertile and his speed of writing so great that, until his death, only two years (1926 and 1931) failed to see a new Pirandello play performed. A scant five weeks sufficed for the composition of both his most renowned dramas—*Sei personaggi in cerca d'autore* and *Enrico IV*.

The fame that his stories—considered by some (Italians, particularly) to be his best work—never gained for him was now heaped on him by Italy and the world. *Sei personaggi* was produced in 1922 in New York (by Brock Pemberton) and London, in Paris (by the Pitoëffs) the following year, and in Berlin (by Max Reinhardt) and Vienna in 1924. Pirandello's own Art Theater, founded in Rome in 1925, performed his plays in Italian in the great cities of western and central Europe, North and South America.

By the middle twenties, Pirandello was unquestionably the leading active literary figure in Italy; and, although various countries had their own luminaries (Shaw in England, O'Neill in the United States, etc.), he probably enjoyed the most considerable international reputation of any living dramatist. At home, he suffered none of the restrictions imposed by the Mussolini regime that hampered many other artists. An ardent fascist, and more especially a fervent supporter of the Italian dictator, he even indulged in the melodramatic gesture of donating his Nobel Prize medal to be melted down for guns at the time of the invasion of Ethiopia.

Eric Bentley states that "under fascism, Pirandello's playwriting entered a . . . problematic phase." [2] Indeed, many of his later plays lack his former dramatic flair, weighted down as they are by ponderous symbolism. However, fascist ideology is apparent in only two works, in "the anti-liberal animus of *The New Colony* and the miracle-mongering of *Lazarus*." [3]

Luigi Pirandello died in Rome on December 10, 1936, leaving behind forty-three plays, collected under the title *Maschere nude,* six novels, more than two hundred and fifty short stories, and various bits of criticism and poetry. He had been an unhappy man in a life dominated by tragedy. His financial tribulations, his wife's illness, the prolonged non-success of his writings all helped form his pessimistic outlook on life, although these factors did develop in him understanding and pity. Even success held no happiness for him. In his play *Quando si è qualcuno,* he described the ravages of fame. Pirandello was an extremely introspective, withdrawn man who found an outlet, but no relief, in his art.

The world paid homage to the man who had rejuvenated the theater, modernized out-dated decadent literature by stressing the pessimistic over the sensual, and brought relativism to the stage. His place in twentieth-century Italian letters is unique. In the history of the stage, he ranks as the greatest innovator since Ibsen, a truly towering figure in the modern theater.

It was not, however, until December 20, 1922, that a Pirandello play was first performed in Paris. Although *Six Characters in Search of an Author* had already triumphed in London and New York, and the twenty-four plays already produced in Italy had established Pirandello's position at the head of his country's men of the theater, the Italian author was still unknown in France.

Charles Dullin was seeking an Italian play for the 1922–

1923 season, and he wrote to Madame Camille Mallarmé, well known for her interest in things Italian, asking her to select one—perhaps by Verga. Instead, she got in touch with Pirandello. His suggestion of *Così è (se vi pare)* for his first Parisian performance was rejected by Madame Mallarmé, and *Il Piacere dell'onestà* was finally chosen. Madame Mallarmé translated the play,* and on December 20, *La Volupté de l'honneur* was created at the Théâtre de l'Atelier.[4] In the words of Marcel Achard, *La Volupté de l'honneur* "struck like a bolt of lightning. Dullin was extraordinary as Baldovino, and the unusual tone created by the play made the critics sit up and take notice. . . ."[5]

Yet, in the history of the French theater, not *La Volupté de l'honneur* but *Six Personnages en quête d'auteur (Sei personaggi in cerca d'autore)* became the great revelation of Pirandellism. The primary reason is undoubtedly the difference in the character of the plays: the former neither has the dramatically striking qualities of the latter nor is it so much of an innovation. Then, too, there was Benjamin Crémieux's excellent translation, as well as the extraordinary acting and production of that memorable evening. If *La Volupté de l'honneur* struck like a bolt of lightning, *Six Personnages* had the effect of an earthquake.

> Georges Pitoëff's phantom-like aspect [as the Father], his diction, so strange that it seemed supra-terrestrial, Ludmilla Pitoëff's communicative emotion in the role of the daughter, Michel Simon's extraordinary portrait of the director, but above all Benjamin Crémieux's limpid and admirable translation caused the play's triumph.

---

* Madame Mallarmé's translation is rather poor. It lacks both the force and the accuracy of Benjamin Crémieux's translations. Fortunately for the French public, it was Crémieux who became Pirandello's regular translator until his death at the hands of the Germans during the war. Crémieux was the outstanding critical link to Italian literature in France.

Georges had had the brilliantly bizarre idea of utilizing the elevator, usually used to bring furniture down from the flies, to bring the family of characters onto the stage. This director's trick (which no one has ever been able to duplicate) left all the spectators amazed and elated.[6]

The date of this first performance at the Comédie des Champs-Elysées was April 10, 1923, and it marked the beginning of Pirandello's conquest of Paris. Critics and public alike were enthusiastic over this strange "comedy in the making." Pierre Brisson wrote that the Pitoëff company

resounded a thunderous peal whose reverberations were considerable by presenting on the small stage of the [Théâtre des] Champs Elysées *Six Characters in Search of an Author.*

Overnight, Pirandello conquered his reputation as a sorcerer of dramatic art. It was a window suddenly opened, a flood of dreams freshly clothed on the stage.[7]

And Brisson said in his collection of reviews, *Au Hasard des soirées:* "It is clear that a play such as *Six Characters* marked a new achievement in the contemporary history of the theater." [8]

The play did, in fact, introduce an entirely new element to the French stage. Pirandello had gone to the very heart of the drama, displaying a technique at once boldly modern and immediately comprehensible. Critic Henri Beraud exclaims that the work "overwhelmed my soul. It is one of the strongest, strangest, most daring and most ingenious plays I have ever been able to hear." [9] Armand Salacrou reacted similarly to the play: "Its evident strangeness had captivated me and I had been overwhelmed by the spectacle." [10] Dullin first brought Pirandello to France, but Pitoëff was most responsible for the gigantic success that the Italian was to have in France.

In October, 1924, it was Dullin's turn to score at the Atelier with *Così è (se vi pare),* translated—by Crémieux, this time—as

Chacun Sa Vérité. With the director playing Laudisi and his wife Signora Frola, *Chacun Sa Vérité* was also acclaimed, and Parisian audiences gained further insight into the subtle interplay of reality and illusion. With it, Dullin also produced a one-act play by Pirandello, *L'Imbécile (L'Imbecille)*.

Early in 1925, two important plays and one minor one were performed. Playing the title role, Georges Pitoëff created *Henri IV (Enrico IV)* at the Monte Carlo Theater in January and then, on February 23, brought it to the Théâtre des Arts in Paris. Five days earlier, Madame Simone had given her initial performance as Ersilia Drei in *Vêtir ceux qui sont nus (Vestire gli ignudi)* at the Théâtre de la Renaissance, together with *Diplômé (La Patente)*, both directed by Henri Varna. Dullin's two productions, *Chacun Sa Vérité* and *L'Imbécile*, were still being given at the Atelier, but no one thought that five plays by the Sicilian were too many at one time.

> Pirandello "forever" [sic]! Do you like Pirandello? He is being put on everywhere, at the Atelier, at the Renaissance, at the Théâtre des Arts; he is being played in three theaters at the same time—a fact without precedent for a foreign author; it's a rage, an infatuation, a fancy, a craze.[11]

This was probably the apex of Pirandello's popularity in France. In July of the same year, the author brought his own recently formed company to Paris for a triumphant Italian-language *Enrico IV*.

In 1926, Dullin and Pitoëff each produced a new play by Pirandello—the former, *Tout pour le mieux (Tutto per bene)* at the Atelier on April 12, and the latter, *Comme ci ou comme ça (Ciascuno a suo modo)* at the Théâtre des Arts on May 3. This friendly rivalry over Pirandello was then in its third successive season. The success of these productions was considerable, though not so overwhelming as that of the Italian's great-

est plays. That year, Gaston Rageot wrote: "At present Pirandello is the great dramatist of the western world. He occupies
a place perceptibly analogous to the one whose illustrious in-
cumbent at one time was Ibsen." [12]

No works by Pirandello were produced in 1927 and 1929,
but the Comédie la Croix-Nivert did *Comme avant, mieux
qu'avant (Come prima, meglio di prima)* at the Grenelle on
March 6, 1928. From 1930 until his death in 1936, Pirandello was represented by one play each season in Paris. In
1930, it was *La Vie que t'ai donnée (La Vita che ti diedi)*, done
by the Compagnie de la Petite Scène at the Salle d'Iéna; in
1931, Max Maurey's *L'Homme, la bête et la vertu (L'Uomo,
la bestia, e la virtù)* at the Saint-Georges; in 1932, Gaston
Baty's *Comme tu me veux (Come tu mi vuoi)* at the Mont-
parnasse; in 1933, Petrolini's Italian performance of *Agro di
limone* (also known as *Lumìe di Sicilia*) at the Théâtre de la
Potinière; in 1934, a revival of *La Volupté de l'honneur*; and,
in 1935, Pitoëff's *Ce Soir on improvise (Questa sera si recita a
soggetto)* at the Mathurins. There were some lukewarm re-
ceptions during the decade, but this last play again won
plaudits for Pirandello from the Parisian public. In March,
1937, only a few months after Pirandello's death, *Chacun Sa
Vérité* was revived at the Comédie Française; and, in 1941,
André Barsacq brought back *Vêtir ceux qui sont nus* at the
Atelier.

The war put a temporary halt to these revivals and to new
performances, but the midcentury has seen a great spurt of
activity. In 1950, Jacques Mauclair produced the French
premières of three one-acters, *Cécé (Cecè), Je rêvais (peut-être)
(Sogno [ma forse no]),* and *La Fleur à la bouche (L'Uomo dal
fiore in bocca),* in translations by Crémieux's widow, Marie-
Anne Comnène, who ably continued her husband's work.
That same winter, Jean Vilar, who has since become one of

France's leading *metteurs-en-scène* with his Théâtre National Populaire, triumphed with a revival of *Henri IV*.

In 1951, *Chacun Sa Vérité* was made part of the permanent repertory of the Comédie Française, joined the following year by *Six Personnages en quête d'auteur*. Two premières were held in 1952: *Méfie-toi, Giacomino (Pensaci, Giacomino!)* and *La Jarre (La Giara)*, produced by Jean-Marie Serreau at the Babylone. There were two more revivals in 1953, *Comme tu me veux* and *Tout pour le mieux,* and a première in 1954, *Bellavita (Bellavita)* at the Petit Marigny. More recent performances of Pirandello in Paris were a successful revival of *La Volupté de l'honneur* by Jean Mercure in 1955, *Comme avant, mieux qu'avant* at the Théâtre de Paris in 1956, Sacha Pitoëff's *Ce Soir on improvise* late in 1957, and the inclusion in that same year of *Henri IV* in the repertory of Jean Vilar's Théâtre National Populaire. This sizable total of fourteen different plays in the space of a few years attests to a continuing, and perhaps increasing, interest in Pirandello.

Not long before this flood of the Sicilian's plays inundated the Parisian stage for the second time in less than thirty years, Marcel Doisy prophetically concluded his study of the contemporary French theater:

> But the most important thing we owe Dante's homeland is Pirandellism. . . . Surely no man of the theater since Ibsen had given Europe so totally renewed conceptions of the theater, a more violently original artistry together with so personal a technique. . . . And it certainly seems as if his revelations are still far from being exhausted. . . . Pirandello might easily remain one of the guiding lights of the period which is opening.[13]

This statement has been borne out not only by the production of these fourteen plays within a decade, but also, as we shall see, by the young contemporary French dramatists whose works reflect the still-potent qualities of Pirandello's theater.

In the years since Dullin's and Pitoëff's startling revelations of his talent, Pirandello has become as much a part of the French scene as he was of the Italian. It is commonly said that he was more appreciated in France than in his native country. Although this seems to be somewhat exaggerated, for Italy admires and reveres Pirandello more than any other writer of this century, it is, perhaps, the proud boast of a country which took him to its heart and made him its most popular foreign author. We shall see, furthermore, that Pirandello's plays are now an integral part of the contemporary French theater. No history of it could be complete without due mention of the author of *Sei personaggi in cerca d'autore*. He was certainly the most important foreign influence and very possibly the most important single influence of any kind.

II

The Ideas in Pirandello's Theater

HAVING seen what a prodigious number of Pirandello's plays were produced in France and what great acclaim greeted them, we must now seek the reason for this success. Why were these plays so appealing both to the French theatrical public and to French dramatists? What elements in Pirandello's theater made such a great impression in one of the most brilliant periods of the Parisian stage?

Pirandello's remarkable appeal resides in the realm of ideas. The pessimism and the feeling of absurdity which he created through his dominant themes—the multiplicity of personality and the relativity of truth—struck a responsive chord in his contemporaries. Indeed, they continue to mark Pirandello as a very modern author today, when pessimism and absurdity are the main strands out of which so much of our literature is woven. Setting aside the Sicilian comedies (such as *La Giara*), we are in the presence of a true theater of ideas wherein the author's views of life and art blend now more, now less, successfully with the demands of the stage. It is a theater of ideas rather than an erudite, intellectual theater, for the ideas are always predominant and the dialogue is often of a philosophical nature, not merely "intellectual" in any facile sense. While individual plays have their own force and movement, they seem nevertheless to be ranged within the basic framework of Pirandello's philosophic attitudes. Considering the large number of plays in which these ideas are illustrated, there are relatively few recurrent themes. Along with the relativity of truth and the duality of personality can be mentioned the concept that opposes the ultimate reality of art to the basic unreality of life; a profound ridiculing of society's prevalent moral code; and, finally—a mood rather than a theme —an overwhelming atmosphere of pessimism.

THE RELATIVITY OF TRUTH

Although "relativity of truth" and "duality of personality" sometimes overlap in the Pirandellian scheme, these two ideas are usually sufficiently distinct to make separate treatment possible and, indeed, desirable. The concept of relativity of truth develops out of that dichotomy between reality and illusion which exists at the base of Pirandello's world. It is the basic principle underlying all relationships between individuals, a multiplicity which must be respected if a *modus vivendi* is to exist between any one person and the rest of society. For the truth does not exist absolutely but merely as the product of the endlessly varied conceptions that people have of it. If men are to coexist, they must comprehend this axiom and apply it in their daily existence to attain a relationship with others based on tolerance with respect to verity. When men seek to know the truth about someone or about some event, unaware that there is no single answer to their search, they leave behind them only a trail of shattered lives and torn remnants of laboriously constructed veils which were meant to shelter the faces behind them and give them a desperately needed aura of self-respect—the self-respect without which no one can exist, for it endows the individual with the basic mechanism required to allow a man to live with himself. To keep this mechanism functioning, a small lie is often more effective than a great deal of truth. This lie, provided it hurts no one else, must be respected by others just as if it were not a lie at all. Pretense and deception need not be evil; rather, they can be saving traits, enabling society to operate.

One of Pirandello's earliest plays, the not-too-well-known *Liolà* (1916),* which in its graceful blending of Mediterranean humor and Pirandellian intellectual themes serves as a transitional work between the Sicilian comedies and the "cerebral" theater, illustrates the last idea clearly. The plot involves a simple superimposition of deception, pointing out that the best way to fight a fraud is sometimes with a bigger fraud. In the confusion of women who claim that they are having children by the hero, Liolà, it is illusion which finally triumphs by imposing itself.

Liolà is a gay, charming fellow—so charming, in fact, that none of the girls can resist him. He lives peacefully with his mother, who takes care of three little boys borne him by three farm girls. When Tuzza, who is also going to have his child, wants to pass her yet unborn baby off as Zio Simone's, complications set in. Simone, an elderly and wealthy farmer, not having had a child by his young wife, Mita, accepts the deceitful plan: knowing full well that Tuzza is carrying Liolà's child, he will nevertheless proclaim to the world that it is his, in order to have an heir and prove that it has been Mita and not he who has been the cause of their childlessness. Tuzza,

---

* Dates in parentheses following the name of a play indicate when that play was first performed.

for her part, is jealous of Mita's position of wealth and of the
fact that she has both a husband and an admirer—Liolà. But
the young man will not permit himself to be used for this
kind of a ruse. He convinces Mita, once his sweetheart and
now despondent over her husband's betrayal, to have a child
with him and then say that the child is Simone's. This is done,
and Tuzza's scheme is foiled as Simone is happy to "have a
child" with his wife, while Tuzza is left alone with her
burden.

The illusion is the important thing. Simone's cousin says:
". . . this is not real deceit here. The deceit is in you, hidden
in you. . . ." And Mita agrees: "Yes, that's true; deceit is
where it does not seem to be. . . ." [1] Thus, true deceit exists
only inside people. Deceiving oneself Pirandello would call
a failing. But sometimes deceiving others is perfectly harmless. Zio Simone's fault is in believing his own tale to the
point of trying to show up his wife. But otherwise, what
harm is there in the old man's attempt to prove his virility
to the town? None will believe him anyway, but he can *act*
as if they did; he can create a veil behind which he can live
contentedly, and no one will be the worse for it (except, as
happens in these circumstances, Mita).

Liolà sets about to foil Tuzza's scheme because he does not
want to see the innocent Mita suffer. To achieve his purpose,
he does not go to Simone to denounce the plot—that would
only make matters worse and complicate the situation. Instead, he will prove that Mita *is* fertile, preserving at the
same time Simone's illusions about his own capabilities. Thus,
when Mita tells her husband that she will have a child by him,
he believes it even though everyone tells him it is not true.
He does not appear to be the father, but the town is willing to
accept the fiction. That he *seems* to be the father is enough for
Simone. Tuzza has told him the truth about *her* child; Mita

does not, and this saves the old man, for he is content in the deception. The greater lie, then, has nullified the lesser and has restored harmony.

Liolà, to be sure, is merely a beginning in the development of this theme, which, in this play, is presented only through the plot, without any of the discussions characteristic of the more truly philosophical plays. The year 1917 saw three new Pirandello plays in which the idea of the relativity of truth is more fully developed.

Il Berretto a sonagli (1917), while still Sicilian in its setting, is imbued with a certain bitterness that marks a sharp contrast to *Liolà*. Concerning a man betrayed by his wife, this play also focuses attention on a man's need to display a front of respectability that others will honor, no matter how sordid the truth behind it may be. When the fiction that all is well in Ciampa's marriage is destroyed through public denunciations by his wife's lover's wife, the situation can only be saved by discrediting her. Consequently, Ciampa and the erring twosome declare the woman to be mad, have her committed for a brief period of time, and thereby save their respectability in the community. Once again, it is a lie that enables the outward "truth" to remain, concealing, in that way, the inner facts which must be kept private.

With the same premise as a starting point, *Il Piacere dell'onestà* concludes on a different note. To wrap in a cloak of respectability the reputation of his pregnant mistress, the Marquis Fabio, unhappily married himself, arranges for his friend, Baldovino, to marry her with the understanding that he will be a husband in name only. But Baldovino, unlike Ciampa, is not willing to be complaisant; and, not satisfied with mere appearances, he is soon fascinated by the "pleasure of respectability" and insists that the roles he and his wife,

Agata, have assumed, be played to the full. (It might be noted
that the play ends happily with the couple falling in love with
each other.) In this play, then, the illusion, rather than concealing the truth, imposes itself thereon and finally takes its
place as the new truth.

The third play to be produced in 1917, *Così è (se vi pare)*,
is, perhaps, Pirandello's most extensive elaboration on the
reality-illusion dichotomy. The title itself makes it clear that
truth is relative to the individual interpretation of it. The
play has additional interest because of the character of Laudisi
who is a *raisonneur,* detached from the immediate action—a
creation rare on the Pirandellian stage. Through Laudisi's
caustic remarks and ironic laughter, the author's purpose becomes abundantly clear.

The veiled face of Signora Ponza, at the conclusion of the
play, is quite obviously the transparent symbol of Pirandello's
truth: the truth depends completely on whosoever observes
it. The mysterious woman is both Ponza's second wife and
Signora Frola's daughter, irreconcilable as these two possibilities may seem. It is futile to try to know more, and the
townspeople, who have been expending untold energy to un-
cover the mystery, have not only been wasting their own time
but have been doing a disservice to their neighbors by attempting to stir up a past that was not meant to be disturbed and
whose riddle has no solution.

Throughout, Pirandello keeps his audience captive, induc-
ing us to shift our opinion of the truth as his characters change
theirs. With every new revelation we are led to accept a different version of the truth. First we believe that Signora Frola
is separated from her daughter because Ponza, because of a
mental disturbance, thinks she is his second wife, and his
mother-in-law humors him to help him preserve his equi-
librium. However, when Ponza announces that not he but

Signora Frola is unbalanced, that his present wife is indeed his second, and that the first Signora Ponza, the elderly lady's daughter, is dead, we readily lend him our credence. In a later scene, Ponza, confronted by his mother-in-law, admits the truth of her story, but reverts to his previous tale as soon as she has departed. He did this, he explains, in order to preserve her illusion. The spectator is helplessly lost.

If Ponza is anxious to maintain the fiction, Agazzi, his family, and his friends are only too eager to find some truth, something they can call *the* truth, which will sate their curiosity and provide them with a convenient answer to clarify the chaos of puzzling enigmas. Only Laudisi refuses to be consumed by the thirst for disclosure. He understands that Ponza's reality need not be Signora Frola's illusion, because he realizes that black and white are not the only colors that portray life. Like the fantastic rock formations of canyons, people change their colors continuously and, seen at different times, convey different impressions. The essential wisdom needed—and Laudisi possesses it—is the tolerance that admits the impossibility of seeing all aspects of a given subject.

Having accepted the diversity of truths, Laudisi takes the logical, final step: not only does he recognize the possibility of a multiple reality, but he is also resolved to respect whatever truth people want to assume for themselves.

> They have created—she for him or he for her—a fiction which has the same consistence as reality, in which they have lived since in perfect agreement, pacified. And this reality of theirs cannot be destroyed by any document since they can breathe it, see it, feel it, touch it!—The most the document could do for you is to relieve your foolish curiosity. You don't have it and so there you are condemned to the marvelous torture of having before you, next to you, fiction on the one hand and reality on the other and of not being able to distinguish one from the other! [2]

What, then, is one to do in a situation in which reality and illusion cannot be distinguished? The only reasonable answer is to leave them alone, not to search for solutions which, if they are found, merely satisfy the curiosity of the seekers and at the same time destroy the inner stability of the people involved. Ponza and Signora Frola had established an arrangement that enabled them to live as best they could. It satisfied them, and it should have satisfied the others. But, unable to leave questions unanswered, the others felt an overwhelming urge to find "a truth," and this urge is a basic destructive principle of life, so reminiscent of Ibsen's *The Wild Duck*. The regenerating antidote is Laudisi's position: one should be content to think that *così è (se vi pare).**

The themes of these first plays are repeated in the next few years. *L'Uomo, la bestia e la virtù* (1919) is a humorous blending of the innocent deceptions of *Liolà* and the raucous spirit of Machiavelli's *Mandragola*. *Il Giuoco delle parti* (1918) presents us with another complaisant husband, Leone, who so outrages his wife, Selia, by not paying attention to her love affairs that she contrives to engage him in a duel over her in which he is certain to be killed. Leone, willing though he had been to maintain the illusion of his marriage, is not prepared to die for it, and he skillfully manipulates Selia's lover into his own trap. The lover, who serves as second, is forced to substitute for the husband when the latter is unwilling to fight,

---

* In any discussion of Pirandello's ideas, one cannot avoid the problem presented by what seems to be a play on the word "truth." In the frame of reference used by the Italian, truth has the double meaning of what *actually* exists in the world by generally accepted standards, and what individuals believe, or make others believe, to be their personal truth. Pirandello never intends to elicit laughter from a misunderstanding of these terms. On the contrary, he expects the spectator to accept the existence of these two truths. The gap between them furnishes the material for the basic tragedy or comedy of many of his plays. These same comments apply to the word "reality" as well.

and he is killed. Again, illusion has triumphed over reality; the fiction has become so convincing that it has imposed itself on fact, and, in this case, the creators of the illusion have no choice but to accept the consequences, even though they have lost control of the situation.

La Patente (1919) is a short, inconsequential play, but it is of some interest because of its treatment of illusion, Kafka-like in its absurdity. Chiarchiaro is accused by his townsmen of possessing an "evil eye" and loses his job and friends. His only recourse is to have a judgment rendered against himself by a court, thereby confirming the slander officially and enabling him to profit by it, since people will pay to keep him away. In order to survive, the old man must accept the fiction that has been created for him. The situation is bitterly ironic for it portrays a human being whose sole means of combatting the false rumor spread about him is to live up to it.

The years 1921 and 1922 are most important in the development of this theme, for during that period, Pirandello wrote two plays of the greatest interest: *Sei personaggi in cerca d'autore* and *Enrico IV*. These, the author's best-known dramas, are primarily concerned with reality of art versus unreality of life and duality of personality, respectively, but they are also important in the category we are now considering.

Sei personaggi in cerca d'autore startled the theatrical world by its radical technique, by its complicated, cerebral quality, and by the pitiful human tragedy that is the play-within-the-play. Here we must examine two facets of the play: the relation of the tragedy of the characters to the action on stage, and the problems which confront the Father and the Step-Daughter.

As the drama opens, we are in the presence of a rehearsal of

Il Giuoco delle parti, when suddenly six people enter the theater, walk on stage, and demand that they be allowed to act out their story. They claim to be the product of the imagination of a dramatist who, incapable of finishing his play, has left them alive but incomplete, and they seek an author who will consummate their destiny. They insist on reliving on that barren stage the tragic situation in which they have been frozen.

The Mother, having fallen in love with another man, had left her son and the Father at the latter's urging to live with her lover. With him, over the course of many years, she had three children. Economic hardships caused by his death induced the Mother to find employment as a seamstress at Madama Pace's establishment and eventually forced the Step-Daughter to become a prostitute in the same place. The culmination of the characters' tragedy is the encounter at Madama Pace's between the lonely Father and the Step-Daughter. Because they do not know each other, only the Mother's accidental entrance into the room rescues them from utter degradation. The Father brings his wife and her children to his house, but humiliation and resentment are the only emotions that exist among them. The little girl drowns and the young boy shoots himself, but the dilemma of the others remains unsolved.

This sordid tale unfolds piecemeal throughout the three acts. The Director, at first very skeptical, finally deems the incidents worthy of the stage and has the actors assume the roles of the six characters. The result is wholly unsatisfactory, because the players can merely act (and badly, at that) whereas the characters *live* their scene. The reality of the latter is but pretense to the former.

The play ends, as it began, in confusion. When the little boy shoots himself no one knows whether it was true or merely

make-believe; the Father alone understands that this suicide
is his reality—the point at which the author's lens has fixed
him:

> THE LEADING LADY: He's dead! The poor boy! He's dead! Oh,
> what an awful thing!
>
> THE LEADING MAN: What do you mean dead? Pretense, pre-
> tense! Don't believe a word of it!
>
> OTHER ACTORS ON THE RIGHT: Pretense? Reality, reality! He's
> dead!
>
> OTHER ACTORS ON THE LEFT: No! Pretense, pretense!
>
> THE FATHER: What? Pretense? It is reality, gentlemen, real-
> ity, reality!
>
> THE DIRECTOR: Pretense! Reality! Go to the devil, the whole
> bunch of you! Lights! Lights! . . . No, really! I have
> never had anything like this happen to me! They've made
> me lose a whole day.[3]

Pirandello very skillfully created sense out of confusion and
then cast the ending into chaos. The sudden appearance on
a rehearsal stage of six people who claim to represent the
unfinished figment of an author's imagination is astonishing.
At first, we are apt to share the Director's view that they are
mad. But as their tragedy is unfolded, their reality imposes
itself on us, reducing the theatrical people to an unreal background. The wide gulf between the two levels of reality becomes strikingly clear when the actors attempt to re-create the
scene recently "relived" by the characters. Authenticity is
totally lacking. The pathetic, tormented people have been
transformed by the convention of acting into mere puppets
bearing no resemblance to their true selves.

The final double death and the ensuing rapid curtain give
to *Sei personaggi* the continuity of a completed cycle: from
confusion to conviction, we are led back again to confusion.
The drowning and the suicide are real, and yet they have
happened before; as the lights go out in the theater-on-the-

stage, the four "surviving" characters are still seen—what will become of them and what place has their reality in the more common reality of the stage? Thus, in *Sei personaggi in cerca d'autore,* Pirandello has used the relativity-of-truth theme not as the material for the plot, but as the foundation for it.

In addition, the situation of the Father is particularly interesting. His tragic truth, as the author has left him, lies in the meeting with his step-daughter, his chief tormentor, who wants to imprison him in this moment. He protests to the Director:

> Now do you understand the perfidy of that girl? She surprised me in a place, in an act in which she should not have known me, in a way I could not exist for her. And she wants to attribute to me a reality which I never could have expected to have to assume for her in a fleeting, shameful moment of my life! That, gentlemen, is what I feel above all.[4]

It is not fair to judge the Father on the basis of this one moment. He may have been unwise in urging his wife to leave him; he may have many faults; but it is not by a single attitude of lust that his entire life should be appraised. The Father's reality is complex, and the Step-Daughter's view is only one aspect of an intricate picture. And yet for her, the Father's reality as she conceives it is the only valid one. The Father knows that we carry within ourselves

> the illusion of being always "the same person for all people," and always "the one" we believe ourselves to be in each of our acts. It is not true! It is not true! We notice it clearly when by some misfortune we are unexpectedly caught suspended in one of our acts: I mean that we notice then that all of us was not in that act, and that it would therefore be an atrocious injustice to judge us only on that act, keeping us attached to that pillory for an entire existence, as if our whole existence were summed up in that one act.[5]

The Father is capable of seeing himself in all his phases and he knows that his life has meaning through the totality of its lived moments and not through the magnification of one of them. However, he also realizes that his step-daughter's concept of his life is necessarily colored by those aspects of it which concern her most. Thus it is that, for her, the fateful meeting at Madama Pace's becomes the focal point of his life, the one act by which a whole life is to be tainted. The Father has one reality for himself, another, for the girl, and still others for the other characters; his own view may be the most tolerant one, but none is the "correct" one, since truth is always relative.

Enrico IV, considered by many to be Pirandello's finest play, presents an excellent blending of the author's two dominant themes. The confusion between reality and illusion stems directly from the multiple facets of Enrico's personality. Enrico is not "real" at any *one* time, but only in a composite view of his development. In the same way, there is no reality in any one of his acts unless it is seen in the perspective of his entire life.

For a moment, at the outset of the play, the illusion is complete. The scene is the throne room of the eleventh-century German king, Henry the Fourth. When men dressed in costumes of the time appear, the first impression is that of witnessing a historical drama. But, suddenly, a brief dialogue breaks the spell and transports the action to the present day:

> FIRST VALET: Do you happen to have a match, please?
> LANDOLFO: Say! No pipes allowed here!
> FIRST VALET (while Arialdo lights a match and offers it to him): No. I'm smoking a cigarette.[6]

These costumed men are then revealed as private counselors to "King Henry the Fourth of Germany," who had fallen from a horse at a pageant where he was masquerading as that

Teutonic monarch. His mind injured by his fall, he has spent the last twenty years in the belief that he is the king he had impersonated.* In an effort to make his life as pleasant as possible, his wealthy sister has surrounded him with period furnishings and has employed men to act as his court. Thus has Enrico been living all these years in a world constructed entirely of fantasy. Even his visitors must disguise themselves and assume in their speech some fitting historical part.

On the day the play takes place, his visitors are Donna Matilde, a marchesa with whom Enrico had been in love and who had ridden next to him at the tragic pageant; Tito Belcredi, her lover, a sarcastic, quarrelsome man; Frida, the marchesa's daughter, who is the image of her mother twenty years earlier; her fiancé, the Marquis Carlo di Nolli; and Doctor Genoni, a physician come to attempt to cure the madman.

They assume historical roles and are granted an audience by Enrico, who immediately mistrusts Belcredi, as though he intuitively recognizes the man who now has the affections of the woman he once possessed. Matilde even feels that he recognizes her for an instant. Addressing her, Enrico discourses for some time about the lengths to which people will go to look as they did in their youth. His views concern the pretense that the individual requires to protect himself from his own reality:

> . . . we all insist on clinging to our ideas of ourselves, just as a person who is growing old dyes his hair. What difference does it make that, as far as you are concerned, the color of my dyed hair cannot be the true color of my hair?—You, my lady, certainly don't dye yours to deceive others, nor to deceive yourself, but only to deceive a little—a very little bit—your

---

* At no time in the play is the main character referred to by any name other than Enrico IV.

image before the mirror. I do it as a joke. You do it seriously.
But I assure you that despite your being serious about it, you
too are masked, my lady. . . . I am only talking about the
memory which you want to fix for yourself artificially of your
blond hair which you once liked; or of your dark hair if you
used to have dark hair: the fading image of your youth.[7]

The Doctor, convinced in his dogmatism that Enrico is mad,
evolves a plan: Frida will don the dress her mother had
worn for a portrait that hangs in the throne room. The young
girl will, in fact, take the place of the portrait and call to
Enrico. At that moment, Matilde too will appear, and Enrico,
confronted with his love as she was then and as she is now,
will realize (according to the Doctor) that twenty years have
passed and come back to his senses.

But at the end of Act II, Enrico suddenly tells his servants
that he is not mad at all, that, indeed, he has not been mad
for the past eight years. He has been acting his role consciously, living in a world that had become real for him.

The execution of the Doctor's plot so shocks him that he is
almost dispatched back to the realm of insanity, but he manages to control himself sufficiently to confront the others with
the truth, which he is no longer able to keep secret. Upon re-
gaining his senses years ago, he explains, he found that the
world held nothing more for him. Everyone but he had
progressed twelve years. Matilde had replaced him with
Belcredi. And thus he had reverted to the eleventh-century
world in which he felt much more at home. He further reveals that Belcredi, out of jealousy, had pricked his horse
while riding behind him at the pageant, thus causing the misfortune. In a fit of rage, Enrico takes his sword and kills
Belcredi. He then surrounds himself with his servants and,
horrified that his masquerade has led him to murder, retreats
to the shelter of his imaginary life.

The basic aspects of the plot of *Enrico IV* read like a case history of amnesia compounded with schizophrenia. Again reality and illusion are intricately intertwined by the complexity of Enrico's personality pattern. The historically accurate surroundings in which he is placed are illusion, because they are contrived. And yet for Enrico they are the only reality for twelve years of delusion—so real in fact that, when he regained his senses, the illusion became reality, and reality mere illusion, because the outside world had lost all meaning for him.

On a different plane, Enrico "voices the aspiration of the individual to create his own world in this storm-tossed universe." [8] He is an individual at odds with society, and he needs his own domain because he cannot be contained in ordinary boundaries. Enrico goes back to the world of madness because the world of actual experience has disappointed him. And when his one subsequent contact with the outside world leads him to murder, the schism is painfully evident: Enrico must retreat to the world of madness, which alone can afford him protection. "Here, together, here, together . . . and forever!" he says to his henchmen,[9] and the despair reflected in these final words stems from the anguished realization that only by accepting the illusion as truth can he escape.

The truth is multiple because it depends on Enrico's personality, which itself is multiple. The world of Enrico IV is an interior one, stemming from the complex nature of his mind.

DUALITY OF PERSONALITY

The era in which *Enrico IV* was written was marked by universal concern with Freud's soundings of the human mind. Pirandello was one of the first to incorporate Freud's ideas into his theater and thus provide one of the great attractions which the French dramatists were to find in him.

The idea of the multiplicity of the self is a ramification of the notion of the relativity of truth. Just as there is no one single truth, so is there no simple definition of a person's nature. For the self is in a continual state of flux—developing, being impressed by new experiences, retrogressing to linger on old ones, but never remaining constant. The essence of a person can be grasped accurately only through the criterion of the totality of his acts and not through a brief glimpse that the observer considers representative. As an event appears differently to various people, so does the personality appear in different guises, and it is never possible to classify it without considering all the facets. Pirandello's man, then, lives in a world wherein the truth is relative and his personality is equally relative, changing at every turn and affording the possibility of understanding it only from the integral approach.

What exactly is Enrico's personality? It is indescribable. In terms of generally accepted standards, he fluctuates from being a normal human being before the pageant, to an amnesiac, to one who, having recovered his memory, prefers the fictitious world to the real one, and lastly to the masquerader unmasked, for whom murder is the symbol of his ultimate rupture with society in an act of affirmation of his private world. The injury caused by the fall was physical, and loss of memory can be an aftereffect of a blow on the head.

But amnesia is not the only phenomenon involved: Enrico certainly gives evidence of schizophrenic behavior. He does not simply lose his memory. Usually such a loss involves forgetting one's name, not recognizing people and objects with which one associates most closely, but it does not involve loss of time perception on a scale so enormous that centuries are involved. Enrico becomes the king he had impersonated, and this metamorphosis cannot be mere accident. Whether it was

caused by a subconscious desire to escape the present world or
to assume royal authority or by some other motive, only a
psychiatrist thoroughly familiar with the case could determine.
It is clear to the layman, however, that Enrico's personality,
considered in all its aspects, tends in two directions. These
are at first quite distinct. Before the pageant, the man is
wholly "himself" and for twelve years afterward he is entirely
Enrico IV. In both these states, complete unto themselves, he
is at least reasonably happy. But after his sudden awakening
the deranged aspect of his personality is at its most obvious.
The two personalities are now intertwined and overlapping;
and, accordingly, life becomes more and more unattractive,
until, having reached the limits of agony, Enrico commits an
act that represents the perfect fusion of his double personality—he kills as Enrico IV for reasons which concern his
other life.

The problem of personality is complicated by the individual's attitude to himself. Often, as a result of shattering experiences in the world, a person is so disillusioned with himself
that he can no longer bear to live with the image that he sees
of himself. At this point he begins a process that Pirandello
terms *costruirsi,* to construct oneself. This process involves the
adoption of a new personality that henceforth will be presented
not only to society but to the individual himself, thereby enabling him to live with himself. It is pure deception, yet a very
necessary one, for no one who considers himself too base can
endure life. Thus people don masks whose dual function is
to offer a pleasing aspect to others and to give a mercifully
deluding reflection to the mirror that the wearer must often
hold to his face.

Enrico's retention of his kingly role after he has regained
his sanity is such a mechanism. To face the world after a
lapse of twelve years would crush him, and so he constructs

for himself as reality the personality that he had unwittingly assumed in his amnesia. The danger arises when others set about, intentionally or not, to tear away the mask. In *Enrico IV* this happens through the intervention of those who wish him only the best, but the result is the same. Enrico is forced to reveal himself openly and the outcome is catastrophic. Only in his constructed role as Enrico IV can he continue to exist.

Vestire gli ignudi (1922) deals exclusively with a woman's attempts to make herself seem better than she is in order to preserve some self-respect. Ersilia Drei had attempted suicide because she had been jilted by Franco Laspiga, who was going to marry another. Her touching story wins for her the sympathy of the press and of Ludovico Nota, an elderly writer. However, as the drama unfolds, more and more facts are uncovered, which prove her tale to be entirely fabricated. Although what she said about Franco was true, she did not mention the real motivations of her attempted suicide. After Franco, she had become the mistress of her employer, Consul Grotti, who had hired her as governess for his daughter. One day the little girl, having been left alone by Ersilia, was killed in a fall from a cliff. Ersilia was with Grotti at the time, and the couple was discovered by his wife. Thrown out by Signora Grotti, Ersilia then found out about Franco's projected marriage. Completely miserable in her guilt, shame, and anger, she was driven first to streetwalking and finally to the attempt to resolve her wretchedness in suicide.

When this sordid background comes to light, Ersilia is again overwhelmed by her past, and she takes, this time successfully, the poison which will relieve her of her unbearable life. Dying, she explains the reason for her lie. Her first suicide attempt was not merely an effort to disrupt Franco's engagement. She really wanted to die, but in dying she wanted to

cover herself with a beautiful piece of clothing—a fiancée's
dress.

> And so, at least for my death, I wanted to make myself a
> decent garment. . . . In all my life I had never been able to
> have one which made me look good without having it torn
> by all these dogs, . . . by all these dogs who were always
> jumping on me at every street corner, . . . without having
> it soiled by the most base and the vilest miseries. I wanted to
> make myself a beautiful one—for my death—the most beau-
> tiful of all—the one that had been like a dream for me, over
> there—and which just like the others, was torn away from
> me—a fiancée's garment; but it was for dying, dying, dying
> and that's all—with a little sorrow by everyone, and that's
> all.[10]

In her life she had tried to create a picture of herself with
which she could live, but others continually destroyed it.
Finally, she tried to create one with which she could die, but
that, too, was not to be. Saved from her first suicide, at which
time she was at least "beautifully dressed," her garments have
now been torn away and she dies finally, naked, stripped of all
illusions.

It is a very moving, a very forceful play, and Ersilia Drei a
most pathetic figure, a woman who can succeed in constructing
neither a life nor even a death for herself.

La Vita che ti diedi (1923) is another play concerned with
a similar problem. Donna Anna, however, does not have to
create illusions about herself; she must create them about her
son, for hers is the tragedy of motherhood. A widow, she
retains in her heart the image of her son as he had been as a
young man when he left home, although he has been gone
many years. When he returns, changed and aged in his mid-
twenties, she fails to recognize him, and when he dies abruptly, he is buried as a stranger. The son had been in love

with a married woman, Lucia Maubel, who is pregnant with his child. Imitating her son's handwriting, Donna Anna writes passionate love letters to Lucia in an effort to keep his image alive in his mistress' mind and, by extension, in her own. It is only when she is confronted by Lucia's mother that she is finally driven to accept his death; she is left in despair, her illusions and her hope gone.

In Donna Anna, possessive motherhood has strayed into the realm of the psychopathic. She could not equate the flattering remembrance of her son with his changed appearance and certainly not with his death. In order to reconcile her wishes with an unchangeable actuality, she resorted to the fanciful notion that her son was not far away and would return soon. She thus fought off the terrible pain that the realization of his death was to bring when she could no longer delude herself.

La Signora Morli, una e due (1920) can be considered as belonging in the same category, yet it misses the point made in the other plays. The plot is quite pedestrian and resembles a second-rate film scenario. Evelina Morli had lived a carefree, instinctive life with her husband until he abandoned her and their son. She is saved from financial ruin by her lawyer, Lello Carpani, who falls in love with her. Although they have not been legally married, they live as man and wife for fourteen years and have a daughter. Their life is settled, secure, and staid. At the end of these fourteen years, Morli returns and creates for Evelina the problem of which man to choose. She still seems to love Morli, and the gay life she would lead with him has great attraction for her; but she stays with Carpani, apparently out of loyalty and inertia.

Of course there are two Signore Morli, but they are over a decade removed. Although she claims at the end of the play, after spending some time with Morli, that she sees two persons within her because she finds herself attracted to two ways of life, her ultimate decision to remain with Carpani casts doubt on the multiplicity of her personality. That she renounces the gay life Morli promises proves that she is capable of doing without it. Moreover, one does not need to have a dual personality to have a serious and a carefree side. Indeed, a well-rounded personality would surely contain both. Her problem, basically, seems to be the choice of which man she wants. It is quite obvious that she prefers Morli, but probably she stays with Carpani out of gratitude, because she still resents the abandonment of many years ago, because her daughter still needs her while her son does not, and lastly because she is more settled now than she once was and no longer wants her life to be frivolous, as life with Morli would have to be. The theme of *La Signora Morli, una e due* is not multiplicity of personality but rather a woman's attempt to deal with two men to both of whom she is greatly attracted, each appealing to a different *side* of her personality.

In two later plays, *Trovarsi* (1932) and *Quando si è qual-cuno* (1933), the personality problem is again carefully explored. The former delves into the problems that arise when one willingly assumes many roles, for the heroine of *Trovarsi* is a great actress. In a world where people wear masks to hide the face beneath, Donata Genzi dons them for art. Acting in the best Stanislavsky tradition, she lives all her roles and assumes hundreds of personalities with the result that her real "self" has been lost in the shuffle. She knows that her every act is an artifice and she needs to find herself—*trovarsi*. This lack of identity brings about the failure of her romance with Eli, a "child of nature" type of artist, for she finds herself acting with him who is always natural. At last she returns to the theater, the only life she really knows and one which he cannot share.

Donata has become too accustomed to wearing masks to be without one. In order to have a private life, she must first find herself, disentangle her personality from those she has been portraying on stage. But her ultimate realization is a paradox: she can never be herself because she is an actress above all, and being herself means being a host of others. Happiness is possible for her only by resigning herself to a lack of identity, thereby making possible a complete immersion in art.

Quando si è qualcuno concerns a poet whose name is not mentioned, for his renown is so great that he exists more truly as a public figure than as an individual. To denote this lack of true identity, Pirandello uses asterisks to show that he is speaking, and * * * is referred to by others as Maestro.

So enchained is he by the fame his poems have brought him that, in the long run, the inspiration of his poetry is crushed. However, when he falls in love with a young girl, he is moved to write beautiful poetry in a modern vein, which he publishes under the pseudonym of Délago, supposedly a young Italo-American writing in Italian in the United States. Immediately, Délago becomes the idol of the younger generation, which now rejects the intellectual leadership of * * *. Feeling more natural in his role as Délago with his young mistress, Veroccia, * * * is torn between it and his acknowledged role as famous poet and head of a family. When the truth is finally known, he must choose between the two personalities and between his family and Veroccia. He knows that the poetry he wrote as Délago is his best and most sincere and that he feels more akin to the man of his creation than to his real self; yet, realizing that he is too old to *be* Délago and driven by his family, he renounces Délago as a hoax and thus kills all vitality within him. To complete the process of self-destruction, he takes part in a ceremony honoring * * * on his fiftieth birthday, at which time he is made a count. Now there is no spark left in him and he is like a statue of the Great Poet, whom all look upon as a sort of national monument.

In this play, * * * has not assumed a new personality in order to hide the unpleasant aspect of his "real" self. Rather, alongside his old disenchanted self, he has developed a fresh, youthful one toward which he is drawn by all that is living and creative within him. His repudiation of Délago is not an admission of his nonexistence. * * *'s spiritual death at the end testifies that Délago lived. The decision is brought about by the tragic realization that life will not let itself be tricked: it is impossible to regain youth by inventing a young man no matter how genuine the feeling of youth may be. Society, too, will have its way. As embodied by his family and friends, it refuses * * * a rejuvenation which it cannot have nor even share. The victory of life and of the world over the individual personality is complete: Délago has ceased to exist entirely and * * * has turned into an automaton. When a human being becomes someone of importance, his reputation overwhelms and subjugates his individuality, creating a puppet that others admire, a puppet made of papier-mâché and not of flesh and bones—a mask with no face behind it.

FORM VERSUS LIFE

Quando si è qualcuno also introduces us to the third important theme of Pirandello's theater. It concerns the problem of artistic creation and opposes life—a fluid, ever-changing force—and form—the rigid, eternal form of art. The paradox of this conflict lies in the fact that Pirandello portrays art as more real than life because it is not subject to the fluctuations of life and therefore exists forever, and yet he shows art as not alive precisely because it *is* fixed and therefore cannot undergo the changes that constitute life. To cite the example that Pirandello uses when he discusses, in his Preface, the plight of the six characters, Francesca is more real when she speaks to Dante in the *Divine Comedy* than she had been when she was alive; in her life, her reality of one moment was never that of the next, whereas in the work of art it is immutable and thus more real. Likewise, the tragic situation at Madama Pace's is real even though the six are not alive but only characters.

> If the Father and the Step-Daughter began their scene over one hundred thousand times in a row, always at the same moment, at the instant when the life of the work of art must be expressed with that cry, it would always resound: unaltered and unalterable in its form, but not like a mechanical repetition, not like a return forced by outside necessities, but on the contrary, each time alive and like new, suddenly born thus forever: embalmed alive in its unalterable form. Thus, every time we open the book, we shall find Francesca alive, confessing her sweet sin to Dante; and if a hundred thousand times in a row we turn to reread this passage, one hundred thousand times in a row Francesca will be speaking her words over again, never repeating them mechanically, but saying them each time for the first time with such a living and sudden passion, that Dante will grow faint each time. Everything that lives, by the fact that it is living, has a form, and for that very reason it must die: except the work of art which *is* alive forever in as much as it is form.[11]

This form of which Pirandello writes has a destructive effect on life, however. It encroaches on it and interferes with it through its attempt to stop life at a particular point, for by removing the quality of continuous change it removes the essence of life itself.

Donata Genzi in *Trovarsi* finds that her art—acting—has so far taken over her life that she is no longer able to be herself; she is acting all the time. For * * *, poetry has completely robbed him of individuality. As a camera shutter catches the subject at only a fraction of a second of its existence and gives a picture that is not lifelike but only real in the portrayal of that fraction of a second, so is * * *'s life reduced to his function as a poet—The Poet—to the detriment of all the other aspects that constitute the complex of his being.

The foremost expression of the problem of art is in the trilogy of the "theater-within-the-theater": *Sei personaggi in cerca d'autore* (1921), *Ciascuno a suo modo* (1924), and *Questa sera si recita a soggetto* (1930). It is certainly no coincidence that Pirandello chose the theater as the field of art for his demonstration, since, concerned with the problem of artistic creation in general, he was particularly interested in the plight of the dramatist.

To treat so complex a matter, Pirandello resorts to complex and striking techniques: In *Sei personaggi,* there are three levels of existence—the audience, the actors, and the characters who reduce the actors to the status of audience. In *Ciascuno a suo modo,* the plot is given twice—the action on the stage is a foreshadowing of what happens later among the "audience" in the "lobby-on-the-stage." In *Questa sera si recita a soggetto,* the director proposes to have his actors improvise on stage, following a story-line by Pirandello—only to find them so taken over by their roles that they reject his direction and assume the lives of their characters. The actual plots of the three plays are rather uncomplicated, and the situation exposed in *Sei personaggi* has already been discussed.

In *Ciascuno a suo modo,* Delia Morello's bad reputation is damaged still more by the suicide of her lover, La Vela, whom she had jilted for another, Michele Rocca. She does not know what motivated her act until she meets Rocca again, falls into his arms, and then runs off with him, realizing that she had truly loved him all along.

What is of greater interest takes place between the acts, for Pirandello presents the above story as a play within another play involving "real" people. To this end, he portrays on stage, after each act, the lobby wherein the "spectators" relive the action that has just taken place. The announcements for the play state that the events concerning the suicide of the sculptor La Vela will be enacted in the play and that, because of unforeseen events that might arise, the management cannot guarantee the number of acts. In the first *intermezzo corale*, following Act I, the "real life" counterparts of Delia Morello and Rocca, Signora Moreno and Baron Nuti want the performance stopped, complaining bitterly that it maligns the dead and slanders the living. The illusion of authenticity is heightened by the usual chatter of spectators at intermission: ample small talk; comments about the play; the sneers of the drama critics; the approval by Pirandello's supporters.

This attempt to create a reality beyond the usual stage action and supposedly on a level of existence with the *actual* audience, leads to the second *intermezzo*, which forces itself upon the stage and puts an end to the play. The scene is the lobby where the ticket takers report that Act II has just ended but that the actors are not coming out for a bow. Signora Moreno has slipped backstage and shouts of great confusion can be heard through the closed curtain. Soon there is bedlam in the lobby. Signora Moreno has slapped the actress playing Delia Morello, causing the latter to depart for home in a huff. The rest of the cast protests that they too will not continue because of this outrage. Nuti and Signora Moreno are also heard complaining bitterly. But suddenly they see each other, address one another in almost the exact terms used by Delia and Rocca in Act II, and finally fall into each other's arms. At last the stage manager and the theater's treasurer are forced to urge the spectators to go home because of the disturbance, which makes it impossible to present the third act that evening.

Again there are three levels of reality: the highest is ours as spectator and reader; the lowest, that of the play excluding the interludes; and between the two, the audience and actors as they appear in the lobby-on-the-stage. The action of the interludes serves to mirror that of the play itself. It is life and the play is form, each having its purpose and each its good features. By seeing a few moments of their lives crystallized before them, given the eternity that only art can bestow, Baron Nuti and Signora Moreno have been able to see clearly into themselves and determine what their true feeings are. The mirror has told the truth, and the two leave together. This is the affirmation of the fluidity of life, which even forces the discontinuation of the play, whose rigidity will not permit it to follow the reunited couple. The dramatist can merely create a situation. He must adhere to it and cannot change it as the lives of the people he is portraying change.

Moreover, the dramatist is hindered by the fact that his art depends also on actors and directors. In *Ciascuno a suo modo,* the temperament of the actors interferes with the play. In *Sei personaggi,* the problem is even more basic, for actors, no matter how competent they may be, are nonetheless acting and not living their roles. When the characters relive their drama on the stage, they suffer with all the poignancy of reality. But the actors' attempt to reconstruct the scene, based on the director's ideas, turns out to be completely false and devoid of any genuine emotion. These are factors with which the dramatist must contend, factors that render his impossible task of creating life on a stage even more difficult.

The title of the play is itself paradoxical, since the six people who materialize on stage are characters, that is to say, figments of Pirandello's imagination. He has, as he states in his Preface, rejected them by refusing to put them in a play where their existence as characters belongs. However, once sprung from his mind, the six assume their own lives, which, at present, exist only in the brief, tragic scene that Pirandello had conceived. As they appear to us on stage, they need someone to finish their play in order to liberate them. But they will not find an author, having already been rejected by their creator. Their fate as characters is to be fixed in but one moment of the existence that is supposed to be theirs. The great power of the artist is to fix his creations forever, but his shortcoming is that by fixing them he finds it impossible to give them life.

What then of improvisation? Would not that art be capable of reproducing the fluidity of life? This is the theme of *Questa sera si recita a soggetto*. The director, Doctor Hinkfuss, wishes to present an improvisation on a tale of Pirandello. He has outlined the plot to his company and agreed on the basic story with them.

The tale that unfolds is one of jealousy. The family La Croce is composed of an elderly father, who makes himself ridiculous by courting a young café singer, and his wife and four daughters, whose free association with men is close to prostitution. The Father is killed in a brawl at the café, and Mommina, one of the girls, marries Rico Verri against the advice of the rest of the family. Verri, consumed by suspicion, locks her up and keeps her from her family and the outside world, with only her baby to keep her company. He is jealous of all the men she has known and, although he has completely crushed her emotionally, he still aspires to dominate her thoughts and even her dreams. Finally, in despair, Mommina dies.

The interesting element of the play is the attitude of the actors. They wrangle constantly with Hinkfuss, protesting that they want either a regular script or a free hand. The director tries to save face before the audience by pretending that this is precisely the effect he wanted, but when the cast finally forces him to withdraw entirely, his defeat is apparent. The actors, who had previously argued bitterly among each other, now throw themselves into their parts with such gusto that the actress playing Mommina faints as she dies on stage. At last, Hinkfuss comes back on stage to proclaim the success of his experiment, although it is obvious by now that what the actors had represented was not an improvisation but a real-life situation.

Again we start out with three levels of reality: the audience; the actors and Hinkfuss; and the characters in the play. These are kept quite distinct at first by the arguments between the actors and the director and by the frequent asides that the latter addresses to the public. But the actors are carried away more and more by the momentum of the story until, after their revolt, they eventually *become* the people of the story. The spell is broken only with Mommina's death, when they revert to their primary function as actors and Dr. Hinkfuss returns to the stage.

We can conclude then that improvisation does not offer the dramatist the possibility of creating life any more than does the regular play. The story of the La Croce family becomes alive only *after* Hinkfuss is cast aside and the actors are completely dominated by their roles and play—or, rather, live—according to their own impulsion. In other words, the play comes alive when all the theatrical elements are discarded: the author, the director, and the actors. The premise of the triumph of a play's situation over the theater itself is an impossible one. It cannot be; and, once again, the playwright is blocked in his attempt to reconcile art and life.

An interesting colloquy on the opposition between form and life—the form no longer represented by the theater but by sculpture—appears in *Diana e la Tuda* (1927). To Sirio Dossi, who is sculpturing a statue of Diana, using the beautiful Tuda as his model, nothing matters but art. His burning desire is to immortalize Tuda's beauty in art, and, with the work still unfinished, he is disturbed to find her changing continuously. Although she loves him, Dossi does not think of her as a person but only as a model. To appease her he marries her, but he deliberately makes her suffer so that he can duplicate her torment in his Diana. The unhappy girl finally leaves him, and when he finds her again she has changed so much that she is no longer Diana. When Dossi admits to his friend and fellow sculptor, Nono Giancano, that he was cruel to Tuda in order to improve his statue, Giancano, who loves Tuda, becomes wild with rage and strangles Dossi to death.

The two artists represent two divergent points of view. Giancano no longer sculptures and he regrets that he ever did because his statues, by fixing their models forever, have robbed them of life, which is constant flux. Dossi is just the opposite. Like an anti-Pygmalion, he draws the life out of his model in an attempt to force the fluidity out of life. Nothing matters to him except the work of art, the ultimate reality whose attainment is worth any and all sacrifices. His victim is life—la Tuda —for he will not allow it to encroach on what alone has value —Diana, or art. For Giancano on the other hand (and he is Pirandello's *porte parole*), Tuda the woman matters much

more than the statue she could become. He feels "that humanity is caught in a trap, the trap of existence, and that our lives
are only a slow and painful progression towards death; to him
the most precious thing in the world is just to be alive." [12]

It may be said in conclusion that one of Pirandello's basic
themes is the eternal opposition of life and form, the latter
unchanging and eternal, the former vital and continuously
fluctuating. The pursuit of life, not the search for form, must
be the human endeavor, since the basic condition of human
existence is one of vitality and change. The two principles are
mutually exclusive: form tends to encroach on and stifle life,
while life, by sometimes imposing itself on form, changes it
from inert to living matter.

MORALITY

Pirandello's theater is, then, principally one of discussion
wherein three main ideas are evaluated: the relativity of truth
as seen from a pragmatic point of view; the concept of multiple
personality that recognizes the many different individuals possible in each of us; and the notion that art or form is essentially
opposed to life. As a by-product of these psychological debates,
the author's views of morality are brought to light—an un-
orthodox morality that can best be described as relative.

Although Pirandello carefully avoids the temptation to
establish himself as judge, his preferences are nevertheless
discernible. In his world of suffering humanity, he would
seem to subscribe to whatever action relieves misery. There is
no absolute standard beyond the need to apply the rule of
"hurt not thy fellow man" to each individual case.

Thus truth, for instance, is not a virtue *per se*. In the
tradition of *The Wild Duck* (which is mentioned again only
because its theme, as expounded by Relling, the *raisonneur*,

is so similar to Pirandello's views), the truth is often too painful to be told and better remains unknown. In *Liolà* and *L'Uomo, la bestia e la virtù* everything ends happily only because the truth is meticulously withheld from those it would destroy. Compare to this the tragedy of *Non si sa come* (1935) in which Romeo, in a moment of sudden and inexplicable passion, betrays his best friend, Giorgio, by seducing his wife, Bice. The woman feels no remorse afterward. She was swept away for an instant, but she attaches no sentimental value to her act and, in fact, still loves only her husband. Romeo, however, is consumed by remorse and drives himself to confess to Giorgio, who, incapable of understanding, kills Romeo in anger. Romeo's sin would have remained harmless had he not insisted on expiation through revelation. Bice's outlook was the only sensible one, for she wanted to forget what had happened in order to spare Giorgio. The truth served no other function than that of catalyst for tragedy.

We have noted the means used in *Così è (se vi pare)* to safeguard the elaborate structure of illusions preserving the secret that must not be known. In *Vestire gli ignudi*, the truth is so unbearable for Ersilia Drei that, stripped of the garments of fancy she had tried to don, she cannot find self-respect even in death. On the other hand, the mother in *La Vita che ti diedi* had to be told that her son was dead lest she ruin the life of his mistress. Right and wrong must be considered in each case individually, for what is good in one circumstance need not be so in another.

This casuistry applies equally to problems other than that of truth. Baldovino of *Il Piacere dell'onestà* is employed as a mere puppet when he marries his friend's mistress, Agata. His sole task is to legitimize the child she is bearing. He soon feels, however, that this pretense is worthy neither of Agata nor of himself, and he steers the marriage toward respectability. In direct contrast is the behavior of Professor Toti in *Pensaci, Giacomino!* (1916). The old man seeks revenge on the government, which has never appreciated the devotion and hard work that he has brought to his schoolroom. To achieve his end, he marries a young, pregnant girl with the understanding that her lover, Giacomino, shall continue in this role. Toti does not in any way think of himself as a husband; the only purpose of his act is to force the government to pay the girl a pension after he dies. Different again is the reaction of Leone Gala of *Il Giuoco delle parti*. His complaisance about his wife's lover is so genuine that she becomes enraged at so much indifference and contrives to have herself insulted by an excellent swordsman so that Leone will be killed defending her honor. But at this point his unconcern reaches a limit, and, claiming that it now falls to the lover to uphold her reputation, Leone calmly sends his rival to the death destined for himself. In each case the remedy for the wrong is different; in each case it is appropriate to the circumstances.

Lastly let us consider the Father's act of sending his wife away with another man in *Sei personaggi*. Despite the Step-Daughter's bitter denunciation of this deed as depraved, the Father was motivated only by a desire for doing good. The project ended in disaster, but it need not have. After the lover's death, the Mother had only to contact her husband for financial help to avoid the subsequent happenings. The Father's action cannot be judged by its outcome; in its conception it stands as a moral act intended for the general good. To be sure, it would not stand the test of universality, but even the Golden Rule must be applied to each case. The situation confronting the characters is a highly individual one, and the solution has no meaning outside its framework. The Father's decision is unusual, but it fits well into the pattern of unorthodoxy and practicality that Pirandello advocates to give some peace to the troubled world of his theater.

PESSIMISM

It is ironic that Pirandello should have considered himself a humorist while the world thinks of him first of all as a pessimist—the perfect pessimist, as MacClintock calls him.[13] Actually, there is no contradiction in these two views, because what Pirandello considers the function of the humorist is generally considered the function of the tragedian: holding the proverbial mirror up to life. The reflections that emanate from this mirror are the shadows of a tortured humanity, the distinctive mark of Pirandello's theater.

Because the plays of Pirandello and George Bernard Shaw are concerned with ideas and have an intellectual quality about them, the two men have often been compared. But the differences between the two point up the essence of the Italian's theater. Both writers possess a ready ability to create remarkable dialogue, but whereas Shaw's sparkles with wit, satire, and a brilliant flow of words, Pirandello's is terse and lifelike, and it is in the situations that his bitter irony finds expression. Shaw's most characteristic plays spotlight social wrongs and human foibles; Pirandello is interested primarily in the tragedy that stems from the confrontation of the individual with his real self. Pirandello is not didactic, but if one were forced to single out a "message," it would be that we must not needlessly force one another to undergo the sorry spectacle of seeing what we really are.

Pirandello is a pessimist because this confrontation is inevitably catastrophic. The men and women of his theater are by no means evil; they are ordinary people, yet the truth concealed behind each is shattering. Suffering is the experience common to all humanity. The suffering caused by others is endurable, but the cry of agony that accompanies the lifting of the masks we wear for the benefit of the world is the most profoundly pitiful utterance of man.

The secret men find behind their own masks is a veritable Pandora's box: baseness, hypocrisy, self-deceit. Pirandello's people are involved in this soul-shattering experience of self-confrontation, wherein the repressed, hidden facets of their beings are revealed. It is at this point that man sees himself in his basic, irreconcilably dual aspects: the cosmic, which he shares with the animals; and the civilized, which he shares only with man. The veil is lifted, and he can see the buried, unresolved conflict between the basic drives and the inhibitions imposed by a society bent on self-preservation.

This revelation is akin to the results of psychoanalysis, with the all-important exception that the physician can carefully prepare and guide his patient, while Pirandello's characters meet their epiphanies suddenly and unexpectedly. As a result, they are deprived of their confidence and self-respect and find life unbearable. Like a scientist, Pirandello remains objective; he condemns neither the code that society imposes on its members nor the natural needs of men. The only partiality he allows himself is pity for his creatures, caught in the trap of existence.

Why is Pirandello's outlook so pessimistic? Why does he conceive life to be an endless and hopeless torment? A partial answer could certainly come from his private life. His unhappy years with his wife must have darkened his outlook; her illness probably gave him an insight into the workings of a diseased mind and of a normal mind as well. His two years as a student in Germany introduced him to Hegel and Schopenhauer and gave him the philosophical training needed to carry his ideas of pessimistic relativity to their logical extremes. Lastly, Pirandello reflects the pessimistic lineage of the *grot-*

teschi and *crepuscolari* writers, who sought to approach the twentieth century with new ideas and techniques, often based on paradox, in order to reflect the complexity, cynicism, and pessimism of contemporary life. Moreover, his plays span the years from the first World War to the middle 1930's, when it was not extraordinary for an author to adopt pessimism as a philosophic attitude. Indeed, many profound writers of the era can be considered pessimistic in outlook.

These reasons, singly or in combination, are responsible for Pirandello's *Weltanschauung*. He admits no truth, no self-lessness, no continuity of personality, and virtue is a quality his characters often seek but rarely attain. His is a glum, hopeless world in which people struggle with the bitter absurdity of existence. Salvation is impossible, and the one ray of hope is kindness, which could make humanity's plight somewhat more tolerable.

Pirandello's pessimism reflected the attitude of a Europe in chaos and of a globe whose values and realities changed abruptly, leaving its inhabitants bewildered and frightened. The French dramatists found in Pirandello a voice that expressed what they felt. For while a generation of Americans lost itself in France in the quest for spiritual values, French writers were beginning to find France (and the world in general) uninspiring, an exhausted spring whose remaining waters tasted bitter.

III

The French Theater: The Nineteen Twenties

In the period following the first World War, the French theater was in a state of transition. Antoine, Paul Fort, and Lugné-Poe had, to be sure, broken the tradition of the "well-made play" and had introduced such modern authors as Ibsen and Hauptmann. But the early part of this century found the Parisian stage still absorbed with predominantly nineteenth-century dramatic concepts: the weightily symbolistic and "silent" drama of Maurice Maeterlinck; the social *pièces à thèse* of Eugène Brieux, François de Curel, and Paul Hervieu; the naturalism of Jules Renard; the romanticism of Edmond Rostand; and the *théâtre d'amour* of Georges de Porto-Riche and the early Henry Bernstein.

The transition from this to the theater of psychological insight of the 1920's, a theater marked by renewed vigor in form and content, is attributable in considerable part to the group of ingenious directors who dominated the scene for two decades. Jacques Copeau's Théâtre du Vieux Colombier gave the French theater not only vigorous plays by such foreign and

48

domestic authors as Gide, Vildrac, and Dostoyevsky, but also actors like Louis Jouvet and Charles Dullin, who, together with Georges Pitoëff and Gaston Baty, were Copeau's successors in the late twenties, the thirties, and the early forties. Thanks to this foursome—*le cartel des quatre*—Paris applauded Chekov and Andreyev, Strindberg, Shaw, and Ibsen, and the most successful of the foreign dramatists, Pirandello. Moreover, these directors mounted plays by most of the authors to be discussed in the following chapters—authors who, consequently, were more likely to be influenced by foreign trends. The theater that was given its impetus by these famous *metteurs en scène* was to enter into one of the great periods in the history of the drama, moving from psychological study to Giraudoux and Anouilh and then to the drama of the absurd of the postwar era—a theater that, in France, is not equaled in originality, scope, and vision by any other, save perhaps by that of the *Grand Siècle*.

Both the critical acclaim and the number of his plays performed in Paris indicate the very powerful impression Pirandello made in France. But the critics were not the only ones impressed. The young contemporary playwrights admired the Italian's treatment of illusions and personality, and they saw the medium of the theater itself in a new light. They adapted what suited their own needs to produce a new theater, whose antecedents rested, at least partially, in Pirandello's. Writing in 1953, Georges Neveux (whose own works will be discussed later) stated:

> Just thirty years ago today, an elevator came down on the stage of the [Théâtre des] Champs Elysées and deposited on it six unexpected characters whom Pirandello had conjured up. And together with them, dozens, hundreds of characters loomed up before us, but we could not yet see them. In order to take shape they awaited the breath of Giraudoux,

of Salacrou, of Anouilh, and of some others. And it will be impossible to understand anything about today's theater if one forgets that little flying box out of which it stepped one April evening in 1923.[1]

Here was the spark that was needed. In Pirandello these young dramatists found themes that reflected the anxieties of the times; they found an exciting technique that brought to the theater the modern forms already adapted by painting, poetry, music, sculpture, and the novel.

> He brought *liberty* to the theater, the possibility of attempting to search; he stylized the mystery which roams through life and which gives rise to so many hypotheses. . . . He appealed to the collaboration of the public's intelligence, he took the public for what it is: an advanced being and not a child to whom one says "1 + 1 = 2, period, that's all." Especially since there is certainly something invisible in 1 + 1. . . .[2]

With Pirandello among those standing at the threshold, the French theater entered the modern age. Cerebral content became an ingredient of the theater, just as suspense and psychological analysis had always been. Pirandello and his successors gave a voice to the uncertainties and the absurdities of twentieth-century life, showing a wretched humanity whose very existence is daily torture. In the mirror that the Italian held up before his characters, the French playwrights saw reflected a dramatic conception with which they could identify. "Pirandello . . . shone in the French sky, and there is not a single satellite which did not retain his rays even long after the passing of the meteor." [3] *

---

* The metaphor is partially to the point because Pirandello's appearance in France was indeed as striking and as brilliant as that of a meteor; but the idea of satellites, because of its connotation of secondary importance, is perhaps ill-chosen.

In fact, some of the French writers were so dazzled by Pirandello—especially by his subtle interplay of illusion and reality and by the technical virtuosity of the "play-within-the-play"—that they went to extremes in imitating him. What resulted then was not good theater but a superficial, inferior copy, "an exterior, mechanical, cheap Pirandellism." [4] Theirs was not a serious artistic effort to absorb certain materials for the creation of new, valid art. Rather, their plays were like parodies taken seriously. Naturally, the unfavorable light of these imitations cast a shadow on the originals. For some years in the early thirties, Pirandello's popularity waned; and, because the French public saw so many facile Pirandellian works, it began to think of him as no more than a clever craftsman. *Pirandellism* became a derogatory term, referring to dramatic wizardry that covered up a lack of basic substance. But, in the middle and final part of the decade, the revival of some of Pirandello's plays combined with the appearance of more good plays showing his influence dissipated this critical viewpoint entirely. H.-R. Lenormand sums up the situation in his book about Georges and Ludmilla Pitoëff:

> A movement of lassitude and of disaffection had taken shape in France with respect to Pirandello. People no longer wanted to see in him anything but a shrewd prestidigitator, a superior entertainer who was supposed to have loaded his dice. Pitoëff never adopted this attitude which seems wholly unjustified. He remained faithful to his conception of the Pirandellian production. What he scorned—what people did not know—is pirandellism, that disease of imitation, that chlorosis of copyists, a veritable epidemic of pale colors which the great Italian propagated among the literary youth at the same time that the public was becoming detached from him. [5]

Fortunately, this negative Pirandellism was only a passing phase, leaving unimpaired Pirandello's importance as the master from whose plays many of the best modern French playwrights drew valuable inspiration. In discussing in what respect individual dramatists were influenced by or showed similarities to the author of *Sei personaggi,* it is only natural that more space be devoted to some French writers than to others, because the degree to which they were influenced differs. To analyze them in categories of 1920's, 1930's, and postwar era is, of necessity, to assign arbitrary divisions. Yet it is not only helpful but quite reasonable, since the French theater, like all French life, reflects a different atmosphere in the thirties as compared to the twenties, and in the postwar era as compared to the period between the two wars.

It seems appropriate to begin this examination with Jean Sarment. To be sure, he does not stand in the first rank of modern French dramatists. Although he enjoyed considerable success, it is improbable that he has left a lasting mark. What makes him a fitting starting point is that he actually "engaged in prepirandellian pirandellism." [6]

Produced in 1921, his *Pêcheur d'ombres* antedates Pirandello's appearance in France by approximately one year. Yet the amnesia-personality theme of *Enrico IV, Siegfried,* and *Le Voyageur sans bagage* is anticipated in the tragedy of a young man, driven to a nervous breakdown and then to loss of memory by unrequited love, who is brought back to himself through the devotion and love of the girl involved, only to retrogress in a tragic dénouement. Basically, Jean's personality is treated in a Pirandellian manner: amnesia is the catalyst for an interruption of a man's personality pattern, and, in the reality-illusion division of his life, the world-as-it-is is decidedly less attractive than the world-as-he-imagines-it, a world of fishing and solitary walks. If, however, the framework calls to mind Pirandello, the superstructure shows quite clearly that this play preceded him. For despite the wonderful opportunity presented by amnesia for portraying a dual personality—an opportunity French dramatists would not be so likely to pass up several years later—Sarment creates no more than an active and a passive facet of the same personality.

While he is suffering from loss of memory, Jean has no real personality. The author treats him in rather clinical terms. No psuedo-Jean emerges in this state, attesting to manifold possibilities within him. This artistic concept will have to await the Italian's conquest of Paris. Jean's regression into amnesia is, then, not the outward symptom of a basic rejection of a part of himself but a rejection of the disappointments that are his life and a search for a peaceful, bearable make-believe. His final escape into death is a violent reconfirmation of his inability to accept reality.

Most of Sarment's later plays have the basic theme of humanity creating illusions to make tolerable a life of never-ending deceptions. Lucie, the heroine of *Les plus beaux yeux du monde* (1925) preserves illusions about her husband because of her blindness; the title character of *Léopold le bien-aimé* (1927) consoles himself for being rejected by women by thinking that he is attractive to them. Thus is it also in *Je suis trop grand pour moi* (1924), *Sur mon beau navire* (1928), and *Le Voyage à Biarritz* (1936).

Jean Sarment's theater, like Pirandello's, is peopled by those who seek escape from life. But they do not turn away from it with the agonized despair and the tortured realization of the impossibility of living it as it is that typify the creations of the Italian. Sarment's heroes are really incurable romantics. If they reject reality it is because they are weak and irresolute. They have vague notions of something better beyond reality. And in their helplessness, their frailty, and their introspection they invariably bring Musset to mind. For Jean Sarment is the modern Musset, brought up to date by an element of Pirandello.

Simon Gantillon's *Maya* (1928) and Jean-Victor Pellerin's *Têtes de rechange* (1926) are two prominent examples of experimental plays of the twenties reflecting Pirandello's multiple-personality concept.

Bella, the heroine of *Maya,* is a prostitute. Into her room come various men and other prostitutes with whom, depending upon their moods, she speaks or is silent, incarnating their illusions. The author endows her with no distinct personality of her own; instead, by nourishing the illusions of those who come in contact with her, she becomes the reflection of their varied personalities. In the last scene, an East-Indian, speaking with mystic overtones, claims that Bella is the same as a bronzed girl he had once seen—Maya, the symbol of illusion.

> Bella, the prostitute, is a symbol of the eternal illusion which draws men to women. . . . Throughout the nine scenes of the play, the woman plays all her varied parts, until one realizes that she herself is nothing, save what is reflected in the eyes of men. She becomes Bella-Maya, the supreme illusion.[7]

In her role—being with each person what he or she would like her to be—she is not unlike Signora Frola of *Così è (se vi pare),* who is both second wife and daughter, depending on who sees her. This conception of personality in its fluidity is entirely Pirandellian.[8] Bella's originality resides in the fact that her mask conceals no "real" Bella but continuously matches the masks of others. Hers is an outward-directed personality in the most complete sense of the term. But the lack of action and lack of substance of the main character, who is merely a reflection, renders nil the dramatic appeal of the play. It is no more than an interesting, not very successful experiment.

Jean-Victor Pellerin's *Têtes de rechange* features a hero, Monsieur Ixe, whose personality is multiple and who lives in constant flux between reality and illusion. In an earlier play, *Intimité* (1922), the author had already revealed a basic preoccupation with the need for escape into fiction from the boredom of life. He demonstrated this by presenting interspersed in a married couple's dull evening at home the daydreams of each spouse.

In *Têtes de rechange*, Pellerin's technique is much more modernistic. The continual and complete interplay of real and fancied situations, the pace of the first part, which speeds up as the lever moves from *Point Mort* (Neutral) to *Travail* (Work) and becomes slow motion as the lever shifts to *Loisir* (Leisure), the fuguelike chorus of rapid dialogue in the restaurant booth as the Opéku of Ixe's imagination dies—these are the elements which classify this play as surrealistic.

Ixe is a young, successful businessman who, during normal conversation with his uncle, Opéku, is transported by his thoughts and reveries to other places, other persons, and other facets of his personality. He considers the work-sleep-eat part of his day the unfortunate necessity of living. Life really exists only in leisure, when it is possible to take leave of its ugliness by plunging into imaginary adventures. This is the realm of valid existence, and, as "Second Ixe" (the second personality of the hero) states, "Real life is never anything but a backward imitation of the other life." [9]

Opéku does not have a vivid enough imagination to live life as fully as Ixe, who has recourse to other Ixes in dream existences. When the chimerical Ixe finds his imaginary uncle dead, he exclaims: "Bah! He has not lost much, he had only one life." [10] In reality, the two cannot communicate with each other because they move on widely separated planes: Opéku is sober and prosaic; Ixe has "spare heads," as the title indicates, with which he can enjoy an extremely varied existence. The play is startling because of its unusual form and ideas. As such it still has considerable interest, if not appeal, today. Ixe is not a Pirandellian character by any means. What is reminiscent of the Italian is Pellerin's entire conception of the existence of multiple Ixes and of a fanciful reality beyond the everyday. These ideas had become much discussed in Parisian theatrical circles by this time, perhaps in part because of Pirandello's resounding success.

Jules Romains is one of those writers whose plays contain distinctly Pirandellian elements, yet one cannot state that he was influenced by the Italian. Rather, the similarities between the two authors indicate that some of their ideas are in accord. *Knock* (1923) and *Donogoo* (1930) are hilarious examples of illusion imposing itself upon truth so completely that it becomes universally accepted. Because this theme had already appeared in *Les Copains* in 1913, Romains is certainly not indebted to Pirandello for it. Moreover, his satirically humorous style and his creations of Knock, Le Trouhadec, and Lamendin are highly original. One might attribute to Pirandello the fact that Romains, after seeing the former's plays, was inspired to reuse the illusion theme, and that he did so in the theater rather than in novels, as he had done earlier.*

---

* In a letter to the author, dated March 15, 1956, Romains writes: "I attended the first performances of Pirandello's plays in Paris. . . ." He speaks of "the admiration I feel for this work and . . . the admiration I felt for the man whom I knew well." He further reveals an interesting project which emphasizes the affinity between the two playwrights: "About 1930 Pirandello and I had made plans to collaborate in writing a play. The preparatory work had been started; but like with many theatrical projects, this one did not lead to anything."

Knock was produced the year following *La Volupté de l'honneur* and shortly after *Six Personnages en quête d'auteur*. The main theme is, of course, a mordant satire against the medical profession in the best Molière tradition. "The Triumph of Medicine," as the ironic subtitle has it, is brought about by the creation of a gigantic illusion which Knock succeeds in imposing on the entire population of the town of Saint-Maurice: he convinces them that healthy people are only sick people who are unaware of their illness and that, in fact, they are all ill. So convincing is Knock that not only has he all the townspeople as his patients, but he even manages to include among them his predecessor, the gullible Doctor Parpalaid.

Written seven years later and satirizing scientists, *Donogoo* is an even better example of the superiority of illusion over reality. When the eminent geographer Yves Le Trouhadec makes a slight mistake by believing erroneous information and describes in his monumental book the Brazilian city of Donogoo-Tonka, which unfortunately does not exist, he risks considerable professional embarrassment; what is worse, his election to the Institute is at stake. The remedy, invented by Lamendin, is as drastic as it is effective. If Donogoo does not exist, it must be made to exist. How can this be done? Simply by pretending loudly enough that there is a city of Donogoo. Lamendin sets in motion a tremendous promotional scheme, which creates the belief that great fortunes can be had there. Naturally, people soon begin to rush to Donogoo, and, finding at the designated spot, isolated from civilization, only a heath and no city, they have no choice but to stay there and start a settlement. Thus, belatedly, is born Donogoo. More and more deluded people follow, until Donogoo is actually a booming city, just as Le Trouhadec had described it. The illusion has become more powerful than reality, and the day is saved for the geographer. He is elected to the Institute, and Lamendin becomes dictator of the South American city, which worships Le Trouhadec as a type of God-hero.

The basic idea in these two plays—that truth is a totally relative concept—clearly shows a similarity to Pirandello, but because Romains came to this idea independently, it is not surprising that his purpose is different. He is not concerned with the philosophic connotations of the relativity of truth. For him, it is a satirical illustration of *unanisme,* and, as such, *Knock* and *Donogoo* form an integral part of his work.

Henri Ghéon is another who may have been inspired by a Pirandellian idea—by the relationship of actor and play—and who has employed it to suit his own quite different purpose. *Le Comédien et la Grâce* (1925) is, above all, a Christian play celebrating the martyrdom of Saint-Genès. For the plot, even for the device of the play-within-the-play, Ghéon went back to Rotrou's *Saint-Genest* (1646); in fact, Ghéon's play is a modern revision of its seventeenth-century counterpart. But it hardly seems accidental that the author should have been led to this old play at this particular time. Discussing the "Fortuna di Pirandello," Silvio d'Amico writes: ". . . Hence we cannot say whether Giraudoux's *Siegfried* . . . or Ghéon's *Le Comédien et la Grâce* . . . or Gantillon's *Maya* . . . or the famous dramatization of Jules Romains' novel, revived in Paris the day before yesterday, *Donogoo-Tonka,* . . . whether all these might be simple coincidence rather than a fruit of imitation." [11]

When Ghéon writes in the Preface to *Le Comédien et la Grâce* that in his play "the character has taken possession of the interpreter," [12] he uses a modern frame of reference, but he is not concerned with questions relating to the fixity of art and the fluidity of life, or with the illusion-reality opposition. He speaks also of the "power of fiction over reality," [13] and it seems likely that these are terms and thoughts stemming from the Sicilian dramatist and not from Rotrou. In granting fiction power over reality, however, Ghéon does not proceed to explore the artistic or the pragmatic significance which this concession implies. His purpose never goes beyond showing the conversion and martyrdom of a famous actor who, playing against his will, the part of the martyr Adrien, is gradually so moved by the character he is rehearsing that, by the time the play is performed before Diocletian, he has himself become a Christian and goes willingly to his death as a result of his public profession of faith.

Genès is a masterful artistic creation. From the beginning, when he is contemptuous of Christianity and requests that he be allowed to play with a mask in order to hide his true feelings, to his initial immersion in the role of Adrien and his moving conversation with his Christian brother to inquire about the sect, until the final scene in which the actor removes his mask and continues in the role of Adrien to declare openly the faith he now embraces so ardently that he welcomes the death that must inevitably follow, the transitions are made so imperceptibly and so subtly that Genès' development from pagan actor to Christian martyr is completely believable. The role has fully dominated the interpreter, and the title Ghéon gave the 1952 edition, *Le Comédien pris à son jeu,* is more fitting than the original one.

Like Ghéon, Gabriel Marcel is a writer in the Christian tradition; but whereas *Le Comédien et la Grâce* treats the positive, the glorious, Marcel is more interested in reaching the disbelievers, the doubters in his audience. Accordingly, his plays deal with a more negative aspect in a humanistic manner that stresses not saintliness and martyrdom but the behavior of ordinary people in ordinary circumstances. Marcel's theater consists of thesis plays, and thesis plays usually make for inferior theater; but the Existentialists—and Marcel is basically an Existentialist—have shown more skill than their predecessors in infusing life into that particular form of dramatic expression. Marcel is the first of those recent authors who have succeeded in creating plays which expound a philosophic point clearly.* Lacking outstanding dramatic impact and theatrical skill, Marcel does not impress very favorably as a dramatist, but his characters are a living part of a suffering humanity and the philosophy he dramatized is readily comprehensible Christian doctrine, orthodox in nature.

It is clear from the foregoing that basically Marcel's theater is not Pirandellian: he used only what served his own distinct ends. "In a general way," states Marcel, "I might be led to say that this whole theater of Pirandello helped me to become aware of what I could call my specific difference." [14] What seems to have brought about this awareness is the spectacle of Pirandello's characters, their masks stripped, observing their images in the mirrors of their souls. This agonizing confrontation is the moment of truth, when man, if he has sufficient strength, can escape from sham. It is this moment that attracts Marcel, and Pirandello's theater focused his attention on it.

Le Divertissement posthume (1923) is "perhaps the most Pirandellian of all my plays," states Marcel.[15] It deals with the triumph of illusion over truth as a dying man's practical joke becomes reality for those surviving him. Before his death, Carteron writes his niece and her husband a cryptic letter alluding to a scandal, thereby causing husband and wife to

---

* The atheist Existentialists of the postwar era assigned to themselves the more difficult task of putting into play form the basic tenets of Existentialist thought.

suspect each other. Their lives become so poisoned by this doubt that they fail to understand the nature of the allegation even when it is exposed to them as a fraud. When he wrote this play, Marcel had already seen Dullin's performance of *La Volupté de l'honneur* but not Pitoëff's *Six Personnages*,[16] and the Pirandellism of *Le Divertissement posthume* may be more coincidental than deliberate.

Of greater interest to us are *La Chapelle ardente* and *Un Homme de Dieu* (both written in 1925). In the former, Aline Fortier, unable to cope with her son's death, attempts to imprison herself and her son's fiancée in the past. She separates the girl, Mireille, from a man she has come to love and pressures her into marrying an invalid. By causing Mireille's unhappiness, Aline feels that she is being true to her son. In so doing, Marcel proposes, she denies the order that God has created in the world and rejects the never-ending vitality that is life. So blinded is Aline that the mirror of her truth reflects only her son. By her persistent delusion, her excessive respect for the past, Aline creates unhappiness—the one act to which no human being has a moral right.

Um Homme de Dieu concerns people who are incapable of sincerity, of asserting the authenticity of their real lives. They are prisoners of their illusions and make each other suffer because they cannot find the path of honest behavior. Pastor Claude Lemoyne forgave his wife's infidelity, which resulted in her only child, Osmonde, now twenty, because he was too cowardly to accept the truth of her love for the real father, Michel. Instead, inspired by what he believes was a lofty act of selflessness and love, incapable of ascertaining the true motives of his acts, he turns to God. Edmée, his wife, was also too weak to accept the full consequences of her love for Michel. Since she knew that she would be forgiven because of her husband's nature, she retreated to security and respectability, thus sacrificing the happiness of three people. When Michel returns as he is dying, the Pastor comprehends Edmée's true motives in begging his forgiveness; and, in his need for revenge, he broadens the tragedy by revealing the truth to Osmonde. The girl takes up the life her mother had rejected and becomes a neighbor's mistress, leaving behind the couple resigned to continuing the sham that they brought about by refusing to accept all reality of existence.

Michel's return forces a general self-examination. The Pastor and his wife see only emptiness behind the masks of their respectability. And they are no longer able to change. Their true instincts have lain buried too long to be resuscitated. Only the next generation is capable of giving continuity to life, and Osmonde's act of liberation stands as the reflection of the act her mother rejected.

In these two plays Marcel deals with characters who lose their identities as true people because they suppress what is true within and beyond them. "The theater of Gabriel Marcel concludes the theater of creatures who do not exist and yet are their characters. . . ." [17] As a Christian and as a man he objects to everything that stifles life and prevents people from living it fully, as it is meant to be lived. He has found dramatically effective and psychologically accurate Pirandello's technique of self-confrontation, which focuses attention—if not always the character's, at least the spectator's—on the illusions with which men and women surround themselves and the world they inhabit.

In the years following Pirandello's conquest of the French stage, three other dramatists were struck by that instant when people gaze in the mirror to see at last what they really are. Henry Bernstein, Denys Amiel, and Henri-René Lenormand treated that instant not with the moralizing overtones of a

Marcel but from the psychological point of view, seeking principles of personality motivations. All three authors had already produced an important part of their works by the middle twenties, but they were impressed by the Italian's bold theater, and each reflected at a certain stage of his career a part of that impression in some play or plays.

Despite his considerable output and his popular success, Bernstein must remain removed from the foremost ranks of French playwrights. He was always a good craftsman but never a great artist or a profound thinker. Whether we look at his early adventure plays or his later psychological ones, we almost always find well-constructed plays that lack sufficient creative spark to warrant a second look and do not leave a lasting impression.

It is noteworthy, therefore, when one of his plays, *La Galerie des glaces* (1924), transcends his traditional lack of real inspiration—if not his mediocrity—to achieve something more valuable, though it is by no means a masterpiece. It is particularly interesting that this more worthwhile play focuses on a very moving and convincing self-confrontation by the principal character—a self-confrontation in the Pirandellian manner, wherein clash the hero's real self and the illusion of the person he thinks he is. Writes Silvio d'Amico:

> From O'Neill's *Great God Brown*, . . . to the very brutal Bernstein, who showed in *La Galerie des glaces* that he was refining himself in the introspection of a man in front of the image he has made of himself, . . . to Amiel's *L'Image,* and to the assorted production of Achard, and also to comical counterfeitings like Savoir's *La Couturière de Lunéville* . . . the name which recurs is always Pirandello, Pirandello, Pirandello.[18]

Charles Bergé, a painter, is tormented. Although he has cause to be content, having won for himself the woman he loves (who had been married to his friend), he constantly searches himself for his truth and finds only doubt, inadequacy, and inferiority. When finally he is assuaged by the knowledge that his wife loves him, he begins to question the importance and the value of love. His personality is such that it drives him to unhappiness while, at the same time, he searches for happiness. He cannot have peace, because his dual nature constantly forces him to observe his own reflection. In his constant turmoil Bergé achieves dramatic stature. He is not one of the legion of Bernstein characters who is rendered wretched by another out of calculation or incompatibility. Bergé comes to life because in this play, Bernstein, like Pirandello, focused on that profound moment in the individual when the mask drops. It is a pity, perhaps, that Bernstein did not remain under the influence of Pirandello longer.*

Neither is Denys Amiel among the first names of the contemporary French stage. In his case, it is not talent that is lacking, for, if he is not one of the outstanding original geniuses of his age, he does have a good deal of insight, ability, and inspiration. But Amiel has a predilection for *intimiste* literature—that literature which, by concentrating on the everyday, the nonheroic if not actually prosaic, almost automatically precludes greatness. His plays, like Bernstein's, have enjoyed fleeting popularity, but one feels that he, unlike the author of *La Galerie des glaces,* could have written more lasting drama. Amiel has stubbornly refused to cater to public taste, however, and has been interested only in expressing what interests him. What he lacks in greatness he compensates for in intellectual honesty, and his theater, although not frequently seen or read today, is still very worthwhile.

---

* It is interesting to note that when the characters in the play go to the theater, they mention that they will see *Six Personnages en quête d'auteur* and that the play is successful (I. iv).

Intimiste theater in general is not in the tradition of Pirandello, but *L'Image* (1927) should be mentioned because it repeats the Sicilian's practice of holding the mirror up to the maskless faces of his characters. The fact that this is not Amiel's usual method and the date of the play would, it seems, justify the inference that Amiel used Pirandello as a model.

Jean and Francine had met when they were very young; they had, in fact, initiated each other into the ways of physical love. After one night spent together, Jean never returned. Some twenty years later they meet again accidentally. In the intervening time, each has pursued, without ever finding it, an ideal of love, seeking always the perfection of the first love, whose memory they have so glorified that they are profoundly moved on meeting again. Having flitted for years from mistress to mistress and from lover to lover, they now plan to live together in the happiness that has always eluded them. But before their first day is over, they see all too clearly that the image each had built up about the past in no way corresponds to reality. In a difficult scene, delicately handled, Amiel portrays the couple after lovemaking. They are disillusioned by each other and by themselves, and each is eager to be by himself. Finally, they leave each other permanently to resume the errant life they had led for twenty years, without, however, the comforting illusion of the "perfect" love they had once enjoyed.

In the scene referred to, as Jean and Francine become aware of the emptiness within them, the idealized image of their first romance is suddenly pitted against the reality of their incompatibility, and in their disenchantment they see only too clearly how sordid and vapid the rest of their lives has been and will be. Their self-confrontation is of the same tragic, human kind that we saw in Pirandello. Amiel's middle-aged man and woman belong to those whose compensating support is torn away when they come face to face with their own realities, leaving behind only loneliness, deception, and resignation. And like Pirandello, Amiel can offer only compassion to his unhappy characters, who move about in life crossing each other's path but never really getting together.

Although his psychoanalytic approach seems artificial and outmoded today, Lenormand is probably the most original and the most important of these three playwrights. His was the theater that brought to the French stage Freudian subjects and outlook. Lenormand explored relentlessly the remote depths of the soul, probing like a psychiatrist to discover the hidden causes of human behavior. If most of his plays leave an impression of morbidity, it is due to what he found hidden in the personalities of his characters.

Lenormand began his analyses some years before Pirandello's appearance in France, but in the middle twenties his method shifted to a study of the basic multiplicity of the personality, along Pirandellian lines. Marcel Doisy, who recognizes the influence of four men on Lenormand—Maeterlinck, Poe, Pirandello, and Freud—states: "Just as the cerebral Sicilian studies the splittings of the self, Lenormand's entire theater tends to show that the unity of the personality is only superficial." [19] Whereas Laurency of *Le Simoun* and l'Homme of *L'Homme et ses fantômes* are simply characters who lack sufficient introspection to recognize the contradictory personality tendencies that motivate their behavior, *Une Vie secrète* (written in 1924 and produced in 1929) and *Mixture* (1927) present us with examples of dual personalities.

Michel Sarterre, the schizophrenic of *Une Vie secrète,* leads a double life. One Michel is a gifted musician, having the power of great artistic accomplishment; the other is a depraved man, thriving on evil as incarnated in his secretary, Vera.

Michel's wife, Thérèse, forces him to take stock of himself, and this self-appraisal is, of course, as painful as it is revealing. With the horror of knowing what he is, his artistry becomes imprisoned, as it were, in his increasingly dominant degenerate self. Vera's suicide frees Michel the artist and destroys his base self as if he had been enchanted by evil spirits and then released from the incantation. This ending seems contrived in as much as Michel had already realized that his difficulty stemmed from within him; consequently, we are totally unprepared to see the blame placed on a vague mystical power—even if Vera is only considered symbolically.

In *Mixture,* however, Lenormand gives full expression to the concept of the multiplicity of personality. On the surface, Monique is the complete, dedicated mother of dramatic and novelistic fiction, sacrificing everything to make life better for her child. In her financial struggle to provide well for her little Poucette, she becomes first a music-hall dancer, then in succession a prostitute, a thief, and a murderess. One day when she is grown up, Poucette realizes that things are not quite what they seem. Monique has subjected her to the company of the scum of mankind; she has left a gun with her in the subconscious hope that she will kill someone; and, instead of marrying her off, she tries to make her become the mistress of a rich old man. Horrified as Poucette is to discover this dual personality in her mother, she loves her and decides to confront her with the truth as a first step in setting things straight. Poucette accuses Monique of having cared for her with rare devotion for the secret pleasure of seeing her fall into vice one day as she, Monique, had. "There is a mother in you," she says, "who wants me to suffer, who wants that I should also endure, renounce, and risk in my turn." [20]

Once Poucette strips the mask from her mother's face, Monique recognizes herself for what she is. With her normal half, she explains the other: "I must have always had a mysterious need for vice, for danger, for fear, and, perhaps, for crime. But since I was too weak to lead that monstrous life without a noble pretext, it is maternal love which furnished me with it." [21]

She acknowledges that she is not only the person she has always thought herself to be, but also another, motivated by strange emotional drives. The conclusion is a somewhat naïve dramatization of the Freudian theory that recognition is the first step in rehabilitation—naïve because the recognition in *Mixture* is the entire cure. Having become aware of her attempts to cause Poucette's downfall, she is at once rid of this desire and the play ends happily. It may be argued that the limitations of the theater justify the telescoping of long processes into a single act, but the play would have better ended on a note of optimism rather than on one of complete resolution of a lifetime's compulsion.

As the title stresses Monique's duality, so do frequent passages of the text underline it. "You are double, like everyone else," exclaims Fearon, the thief, to the mother. "Tell me what is not mixed in the heart of man?" [22] And again: "You make me think of a devil who thought all his life that he had little angel's wings on his back . . . and who suddenly notices that he has a cloven hoof. Bah, everybody has a cloven hoof . . . and also little wings on his back!" [23]

This is dialogue in the best Pirandellian tradition and Monique is not without some tragic overtones of Ersilia Drei of *Vestire gli ignudi*. Unlike the latter, however, Monique changes completely and is able to transcend her tragedy with the devoted help of her daughter, who acts as the play's psychoanalyst.

Lenormand did not dwell on the theme of multiple personality. In his later works he devoted himself more and more to relations between the races and the problem of the half-breed. But he did concern himself in one play with the question of the theater as the channel of the author's expression. Although there is no statement from him to that effect, it is virtually certain that as a man of the theater and as one whose plays were produced by Pitoëff, Lenormand saw the Pitoëff performances of *Six Personnages* in 1923 and *Comme ci (ou comme ça)* in 1926. It also seems probable that Lenormand was interested in these plays, in which the Italian master considered the basic flaw of the theater as an art medium: the life with which the dramatist endows his work is choked by directors and actors who cannot live it but only perform it. In his *Confessions d'un auteur dramatique* Lenormand writes: "What is the theater in its relations with the author and with the public? . . . *Six Characters* is a long interrogation on the causes which can hamper or facilitate the birth of a dramatic work. In *Une Vie secrète* and *Crépuscule du Théâtre*, I handled the same themes." [24]

Une Vie secrète concerns personality rather than artistic creation, and, in any case, it deals with a musician whose creative problems differ from those of the dramatist. But *Crépuscule du Théâtre* (1934) goes to the heart of the problem. As all life is squeezed out of the work by the artifice of the Manager and actors in *Sei personaggi*, so the Author's play is spoiled and stillborn because of bad acting in the first case and, in the second, directors with fixed ideas of what the public wants—directors who take a love story set in an icy, symbolic atmosphere and change it, in Germany, into an erotic jungle wherein explosions replace dialogue, in England, into a children's Christmas fairy tale, and, in Italy, into something else again. The Author is completely unable to have his drama performed as he has written it, and this inability is one symptom of the night which, as the title indicates, is setting over the theater.

Another symptom is the public's indifference to the stage. This, Lenormand feels, may be a result of the first. The director of the French playhouse in which Acts I and III take place fights valiantly to keep his house from being turned into a cinema. But financial difficulties mount steadily. A last attempt to fill the hall, a revival of *The Tempest,* finds only a sparse audience, and even these few spectators are more interested in a boxing match broadcast from abroad. The director capitulates, and celluloid and a screen will henceforth replace the live actors. The curtain falls after a plea for a revival of interest in real theater. The play has the twofold purpose of propaganda for the legitimate stage and of probing, even if not too deeply, into the dilemma of creation faced by the playwright.

Besides the above-mentioned similarity to *Sei personaggi,* there is also a certain similarity in setting and dialogue. In fact, *Crépuscule du Théâtre* begins like the Italian play with an empty, dark stage on which enter gradually the stagehand, actors, actresses, and the director. In both plays, the stars come late for the rehearsal, and upon their arrival the real action begins. It seems that Lenormand deliberately refers in his opening scene to Pirandello's, written eleven years earlier, as if to associate himself with his predecessor's conclusion. There is no real purpose in starting the work in this way; it could easily have *begun* with the conversation between the Director and the American movie-chain owner. In *Sei personaggi,* this unusual opening served a basic function in the over-all conception of the play; Lenormand uses it as a reminiscence of an experience that had obviously impressed him.

The Author's dismay at being misrepresented by the performers is brought out in this colloquy between him and an actress who, he fears, will not interpret her role faithfully. Their comments are very Pirandellian:

> THE AUTHOR: To know that you are here, you, my character, who wants only to live, and to be present at this deformation, this betrayal!
>
> THE ACTRESS: The public does not know your dreams, nor the being you have created. It will accept the image it is given. You will be the only one to feel betrayed.[25]

How reminiscent this is of the debates in *Sei personaggi* between the Director and the actors on the one hand and the Father and the Step-Daughter (representing the author) on the other. Consider the Director's defense of his art:

> THE DIRECTOR: Your expression is only raw material which will be given a body and a face, a voice and gestures by the actors who, I want you to know, are able to express things of a quality different from this. The material which *you* are bringing us is so flimsy that if it succeeds in holding the stage, all the credit, believe me, will be due to my actors.[26]

Or the Father's doubts about the leading actor's ability to impersonate him: "You may then object to me that it is by a simple game that that gentleman (*he points to the leading actor*), who is 'he' must be 'I' who am, in turn, 'that one.'"[27]

The thought is basically the same. Lenormand and Pirandello are both aware that the playwright faces an obstacle that does not hinder other writers. It is a long and hazardous road between the conception of characters and situations in the womb of the dramatist's imagination and their birth on stage, directed by directors, acted by actors, and viewed by a public.

For a short time in his long career, Lenormand seems to have been preoccupied with the ideas of Pirandello. As a man of the theater, he must have been impressed by the Italian's concern for the dramatist's situation; as a student of the human personality, primarily influenced by Freudian principles, he was apparently struck by the Italian's conception of the multiplicity of the self. The literary contact that Lenormand had with Pirandello proved to be a fruitful one in its effect on the Frenchman, injecting new thoughts and attitudes into his work.

The essence of Jean-Jacques Bernard's theater is the unspoken and the everyday. Whereas Lenormand's probings reveal a diseased humanity, Bernard elucidates with subtle and restrained strokes the aspirations and disillusionments of ordinary people. His similarity to Pirandello lies in his treatment of the evolution of those aspirations into disillusionment. The change is often due to the realization by his heroes—or heroines, as is more frequently the case—that their fondest hopes were based on illusions. This is what Benjamin Crémieux terms the *tragique de connaissance,* an element which Pirandello gave to the stage and which forms the link between the Italian's theater and the theater of the Unexpressed.[28]

Bernard is himself fully aware of Pirandello's importance. Like so many writers who are unable to analyze clearly the influences to which they have been subject, Bernard admits that he does not know whether he was directly influenced by the author of *Sei personaggi,* but he does speak of an affinity to him: "I had presented my early plays when I saw those of Pirandello. I therefore could not tell you that he influenced me, but I can assure you that I found myself naturally in accord with his work. As a French author, I consider him to be an author in our family." [29] *

This accord can be seen in three plays. Marie-Louise, the wife in *L'Invitation au voyage* (1924), is captivated by a young man, Philippe, who departs for Argentina and an unknown future. While he is gone, she thinks of him and of the romantic, exciting life she could have shared with him. When he returns, she finds that her notions about him were pure illusion: he is now a settled businessman in Buenos Aires, no more dashing than her husband and not nearly so appealing. The illusion is shared by the audience because Philippe never appears on stage and we know him only as Marie-Louise conceives him. It is a delicate dramatic *tour de force*, carried off by the author with considerable skill.

Brief mention may be made of *Le Printemps des autres* (1924) and *Nationale 6* (1935). In the latter, a simple country girl finds out that illusions about faraway places may be less attractive than the realities around the corner. In the former, the heroine, Clarisse, labors under misconceptions about herself until the end. Commenting on Clarisse, May Daniels writes: "The irony of the drama is in her temporary ignorance of her real personality; the tragedy is in her sudden

---

* Bernard also makes valuable comments on Pirandello's over-all importance in France:

"There is no doubt that Pirandello's work had a considerable influence in France. His works are inseparable from the dramatic renewal between the two wars. We can say today that the name of Pirandello forms a part of the French patrimony. . . .

"That Pirandello, by accenting that eternal truth that a character becomes alive when he escapes from his author, brought a new inspiration is beyond any doubt. . . . In France he appeared at a time when dramatists were haunted, in various forms and more or less consciously, by the problems of the personality. Hence a profound accord between Pirandellian dramaturgy and that of our country" (see note 29).

realization of it." [30] This is precisely the tragedy of Pirandellian characters, and through it a link is established between two authors whose works normally tend in widely divergent directions.

Because Alfred Savoir's *La Couturière de Lunéville* was first performed at the end of January, 1923, its Polish-born author could hardly have been influenced by the French performances of Pirandello—for *La Volupté de l'honneur* had opened only little more than one month earlier, and Pitoëff's *Six Personnages* was not to be seen until April of that year. But there are similarities to Pirandello in *La Couturière de Lunéville*.

In this farce, a liaison between Rollon and a famous American movie star, Irène, is the start of a merry chase. The plot takes shape when Irène's humble origins are revealed: she is really Anna, a seamstress, born in the town of Lunéville where Rollon was stationed during the war. At that time Rollon had seduced her and abandoned her, not knowing that she was to give birth to their child (which subsequently died). In the tradition of classical French comedy, which delights in mistaken identity, Irène disguises herself as her former self and further complicates poor Rollon's life. As Irène, she insists that he stop seeing Anna; as the seamstress, she demands that he break his liaison with the actress. The conflict is finally resolved happily with Rollon's declaration of love to Anna. This convinces the woman that she is now loved for "herself" —although the author never makes it clear what "herself" really is or, in fact, whether she has a "self" or "selves."

The play is a poor one, not even among the author's better plays. The naïveté of the main character is completely unbelievable, and causes the entire work to fall. The dramatization of the duality of Irène-Anna is primitive in its conception, for we never know if it is assumed or real. The final lines of the play are worth mentioning, however, because they indicate that the duality of Irène-Anna (whether real or not) brings to light the dual aspect of Rollon's own personality, drawn to both women as he is.

ROLLON: What? What? . . . You were two?
IRÈNE: Like all women, like many men, like yourself. . . .
ROLLON: Which is your real face? Are you Irène, are you Anna?
IRÈNE: I am the one your desire creates. Anna when I can, Irène when I must. Which one of me do you prefer?
ROLLON: I don't know, I love you, I am yours, because you are two . . . Irène and Anna.[31]

In its own small way, this dialogue is reminiscent of Signora Frola's dramatic appearance that is the culmination of *Così è (se vi pare)*. That *La Couturière de Lunéville* bears some resemblance to Pirandello is about the best thing that can be said for it.

In *Le Figurant de la Gaîté* (1930), however, Savoir is quite consciously Pirandellian. It is a comedy about a young actor who plays bit parts at the Gaîté Theater and continues to live his parts when the curtain has been rung down. In this manner, he is able to lead many exciting lives, assuming in each a different personality and effectively obliterating any personality of his own. At the end, he is offered the opportunity to keep one role permanently, but he refuses, not wanting to be limited to one when he yearns to be many. Unlike *La Couturière de Lunéville*, *Le Figurant de la Gaîté* is very strongly inspired by the Pirandellian concept of the multiplicity of personality, but it is still naïve and mediocre in execution.

The last dramatist to be considered in this chapter is Michel de Ghelderode, a Belgian who wrote plays in the twenties and

yet was completely ignored in Paris until the presentation in
1949 of his *Fastes de l'Enfer* by the Compagnie de Myrmidon
opened the doors to his discovery. Gallimard began publishing
his theater, and a Ghelderode festival was held.

Trois Auteurs, un drame (1926) is as Pirandellian a play as
can be found anywhere. It employs every trick in the Italian's
repertory, and still it is an original play, not a copy. It contains
a play-within-a-play that encroaches on the "life" of the characters, an author who sees his characters escape him, actors
who find in the play they are enacting a resolution of their
personal conflicts. Ghelderode keeps a fine sense of humor
with all this dazzling technique, which he employs with
tongue in cheek. A detailed summary of *Trois Auteurs, un
drame* will reveal the great similarity to Pirandello.

In the Prologue, the Author tells the three actors of his
play—The Heavy Father, The Juvenile Lead, and The
Ingénue—that they have not been doing it justice. On this
opening night in a new city, he exhorts them to greater efforts
in order to earn good reviews. They inform him, however, that
they are doing more than playing roles—they are playing their
lives. Only reluctantly do they consent to carry on with the
play.

> THE JUVENILE LEAD: We knew your scenario before you did!
> THE HEAVY FATHER: We have been acting your play for
> years! [32]

In the "play," set in the Middle Ages, the Duke (The
Heavy Father), elderly and world-weary, recognizes that he
had made a mistake in marrying the young, beautiful Duchess
(The Ingénue). Her lover, the Chevalier Tristan (The Juvenile Lead), tells her she must flee with him this very night
or he will kill himself. More and more their dialogue becomes
permeated by modern conversation fitting their situation, and

they even call each other by their real names, causing the prompter no end of trouble. The Duchess, after receiving a kiss from the Chevalier, exclaims: "You never kissed me so well, Raoul! . . . (*She catches herself*) Tristan!" [33] Soon afterward, the Duke lights a cigarette (an anachronism reminiscent of the opening scene of *Enrico IV*) and departs from the script. The prompter attempts in vain to set him straight, whereupon the Duke responds with colloquialisms totally inconsistent with his role:

THE PROMPTER: My memory . . .
THE DUKE: My memory? I don't give a damn. . . . I will be remembered as a silly ass, a fool, a failure. . . . Guys like me come by the hundreds.[34]

With a final wish that his wife and her lover should stay together, the Duke kills himself. But the Duchess is fickle. Although she would have stayed with Tristan if *he* had killed the Duke, she does not want him now. Tristan pleads with her and even calls her by her real name, "Mariette!" Her answer is the ultimate in intrusion of the actors' modern situation on the medieval "play": "Mariette says *merde* to you!" [35] The double suicide of the Duchess and the Chevalier ends the play.

In the Epilogue, the three actors get up one by one to take their bows. Each thought the others dead, and each claims to have tried to kill himself but missed—inexplicably. To this humorous note, Ghelderode adds a final one: aghast at what has become of his play, the Author shoots himself. The threesome, confronted by the impasse of their triangle, decide they can do nothing but continue.

THE JUVENILE LEAD: What are we going to do?
THE HEAVY FATHER: Continue . . . like yesterday, like always. What has changed? There are still three of us, the way it is in plays; therefore, let's continue to act.[36]

And they all laugh. This imprisonment in their roles is the dead end of Enrico and of the six characters.

The resemblance to Pirandello is obvious. The play "on stage" reflects the action of "life," but since the play is more rigid than life, life encroaches on it and in the end imposes itself. As the title indicates, the actors are the real authors of the drama over which the Author has lost control. As Pirandello had concluded, and Lenormand had confirmed, the author is checked at every point. Ghelderode dramatizes the problem with his mock solution: suicide.

We have seen that there were many French playwrights in the 1920's who found new dramatic inspiration in Pirandello's works. Everyone connected with the stage agreed that the performances of the Italian's plays were a landmark in a changing theater, and the dramatists of the era were naturally very interested in his concepts. In those years when the war to end all wars had given way to what was thought to be peace and it was possible once again (or, perhaps, still) to nourish illusions, Pirandello stressed the reality of illusions. At a time when Freud became a fad, Pirandello examined the far recesses of personality and found what the psychoanalysts found—chaos. Just as contemporary men, individually and collectively, were confronted with this chaos, Pirandello's characters agonized before their own images. Lastly, with the drama straining to escape from its prewar confines, Pirandello pointed to the creative obstacles that impede the playwright.

Thus, the French writers looked to what was modern in the Italian's method and in his reflection of the mood of the times. The dramatists of this decade did not, however, turn to Pirandello with all their energy. With few exceptions, the authors treated in this chapter show similarities to Pirandellian ideas in one or two of their plays only. They tasted from the new spring, as it were. That they tasted is in itself significant, but if many wrote Pirandellian plays, none, with the possible exception of Lenormand, produced a sizable theater to which that adjective can apply.

It was not until the thirties that Pirandello's ideas permeated more extensive creative spans of French writers. By that time, the experimental and novel aspects had worn off; and the essentials of his thought, as it appeared in his own plays and in others that reflected it, were distilled by some of the French dramatists of the years preceding World War II and played a more important role in their total production.

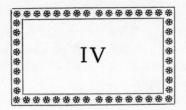

The French Theater: The Nineteen Thirties

I<small>F IT IS</small> to be artistically valid, the theater must reflect the mood of contemporary life. This requirement has been met by all great theaters—that of ancient Greece, of the Elizabethans, of the Golden Age in Spain, of the seventeenth century in France, of Ibsen, Shaw, and Chekov. It has also been met by the modern French theater.

The 1930's were a nightmare for Europeans, and not only in retrospect. Even then it was apparent that disaster was on the horizon, looming larger and larger, preparing itself as inevitably as the tragedy of a Greek play. As the years progressed, political events made it clear that this was not a postwar era—it was the era between the wars.

In this respect, the thirties differ from the twenties by more than the simple number of the decade. The political atmosphere had to leave its imprint on the theater also. Pessimism was the playwright's natural attitude toward life, as, indeed, it had to be for everyone. Anouilh and Salacrou reflected the blackness, and so, to a large extent, did Cocteau. Marcel

Achard's romanticism belonged to days gone by; but Giraudoux, who for years had stressed faith in the triumph of good
in man, acknowledged the imminence of destruction in his
magnificent *La Guerre de Troie n'aura pas lieu.*

In his philosophic outlook, Pirandello never seemed more
modern. By 1935 the full gamut of his dramatic expression
had become known in France. If most of his recent plays
were variations on his earlier ones, his themes and techniques
were still fascinating, and their very repetition served to im-
plant them more firmly in the minds of the French playwrights. Pirandello's works had become increasingly French
to the French, not only because he was almost constantly performed in Paris, but also because his ideas had been made a
part of the French heritage by dramatists of the previous
decade. "The up-coming generation [in 1930]," wrote Pierre
Brisson, "welcomed Pirandello. . . ." [1]

In the thirties, as opposed to the twenties, the number of
playwrights who came under the spell of Pirandello dimin-
ished, but, with few exceptions, the Italian's influence on these
men is more extensive: a major portion of their work, rather
than an occasional play, is impregnated by him. Moreover,
there is greater subtlety in their adaptations, resulting in plays
which, in general, are better than those bearing the Italian's
stamp written by their predecessors.

In a study of Pirandello's fortunes in France, Marcel
Achard's works offer the logical transition from the twenties
to the decade now under consideration. His characters reflect
neither the anguish of his age nor an optimistic note of hope.
They are indifferent to their times and have a life that is
strictly their own. As a group, they are not *engagé,* as the
Existentialists might put it. Like the characters of Sarment,
they are dreamers, poets, misfits in a society to which they

cannot fully adjust—the spiritual heirs of Musset. The Pirandellian notions of illusion and personality fit readily into this
sort of theater.

Achard's attitude is not tragic. His heroes are not trampled
upon by life; their reliance on illusion does not lead them to
destruction; the multiplicity of their personalities does not
bring chaos. Some of these misfits even triumph over life. At
worst they are buffeted around a bit by it, and they arouse in
the spectator that very human mixture of emotions—pity and
amusement. Lalou and Clouard mention Chaplin in describ-
ing that quality of Achard's people.[2] Rhodes speaks of a neo-
romantic revival in the Musset tradition, one of whose repre-
sentatives is Achard:

> Much as it may have become colored by Pirandellian,
> expressionistic and other contemporary dramatic theories, it
> followed, in good measure, traditional lines and forms. It was
> essentially psychological, intellectual, and imaginative in char-
> acter, sentimental with humor, nostalgic with irony, fond of
> pricking and bursting the bubbles of joys, sorrows, and hopes,
> with an art that provokes simultaneously a smile and a tear.[3]

This smile and this tear Achard produces with a seemingly
effortless dramatic skill, which has attracted audiences for
some thirty years. But the period from the late twenties to the
second World War remains the focal point of his career. Here
he reaches his maturity as a dramatist and attains his place as
one of the best of those playwrights who rank just below the
giants of the time.

Jean de la Lune (1929) is the simple, engaging story of
a man who is so trusting and guileless himself that, despite
the most conclusive evidence, he cannot believe his wife is
deceiving him. Marceline is the epitome of inconstancy, and
yet Jef fondly builds up the illusion that she could love only
him. In this seemingly impossible task, he is abetted by as

unlikely and appealing a go-between as has been seen on the stage. He is Clo-Clo, or Clotaire, Marceline's brother, who takes it on himself to arrange the details of her many loves for the sole purpose of protecting, by keeping in ignorance, those she deceives.

Thus it is a completely unsuspecting Jef who learns that his wife is going to leave him. His illusion of her as a pure being is so strong, his complete refusal to believe that she might be capable of deserting him so genuine, that Marceline ends up by becoming what he has imagined her to be all along. She realizes how much she loves him and abandons her shoddy life of flitting from lover to lover. Once again the illusion has proven stronger than reality; the dreamer, the *Jean de la Lune*, has made life conform to his dream.

This basic premise is Pirandellian. Around it, Achard has created a trio of characters and manipulates them with a lightness of touch all his own. Never is Jef's plight expressed with tragic overtones; pity is the most serious emotion Achard allows him to evoke in us. Nor are we indignant at Marceline. She is what she is, and only Jef cannot accept her as such. It is Clo-Clo who really "makes" the play. As his sister's secret assistant, as a parasite unwilling to work, as a basically very good friend, he is a completely original creation. How rare to find so genial a cad! Because of him, one tends to remember the play as better than it really is.

Jean de la Lune was one of Achard's greatest successes, in part, perhaps, because of what has been referred to by all critics as a memorable performance by Michel Simon in the role of Clotaire. But *Domino* (1932) and *Le Corsaire* (1938) are actually superior plays, more unusual in conception, firmer in structure, and—not to be neglected in this study—more markedly influenced by Pirandello.

In *Domino* we are witness not only to a complete imposition of illusion on reality but also to the interesting process through which one man adopts another's personality and molds it to make it become what he thinks it should always have been.

Lorette Heller's husband discovers a love letter, signed François, which his wife had received some time before their marriage a year and a half earlier. He suspects (correctly) his best friend, François Crémone, and decides to ruin him financially. Even though Lorette no longer cares for Crémone and only loves her husband, she is determined to prevent this reprisal. To divert Heller's anger, she hires a young adventurer, Domino, whom she intends to pass off as the François of the letter. Introducing Domino as François, an old friend returned from two years in Africa, she casts enough suspicion on him to confuse her husband. Meanwhile, to Crémone's dismay, Domino has been lyricizing to Lorette about how perfect "their" love must have been. Overcome by the role, Domino rejects her protest that "their" love had, in fact, been quite unsatisfactory: "What you say is true. And yet that is not how things happened." [4] He tells her that François must have been a better man than Crémone, else she could not have loved him. "I was not that nobody, that scoundrel." [5]

In order to impose their deception fully, Lorette and Domino plan to have Heller surprise them as "François" asks her to run away with him. But the husband discovers the plan and the entire truth about Crémone. As he enters, he finds Domino *really* asking Lorette to elope with him. Smugly, he declares that these histrionics are no longer necessary. But it is no act. Having fallen in love with Domino, Lorette decides to leave with him, with the "François" she has always loved in her imagination but who only now has come to her.

Domino bears great similarities to Baldovino of *Il Piacere dell'onestà*. Both are hired to correct in a deceitful manner a dishonest situation. Both come alive in their roles, appropriate them as their reality, and impose this reality on the others. Both fall in love with the women in question and win their love from those who are responsible for the deception. In each case the success of the hero marks the full imposition of an illusion on reality.

As Baldovino's personality, influenced by the "pleasure of honesty," changes to conform to the role he is playing, Domino's changes until he becomes not only "François" but the "François" of Lorette's dreams. First he becomes Crémone by assuming his past; then he transforms him until he attains his greatest reality—that is, until he corresponds to the "François" whom Lorette would have loved and does finally now love. The real Crémone's jealousy is well founded, even though he denies it:

> DOMINO: I believe . . . you are doing me the honor of being jealous of me.
> CRÉMONE: Jealous of you?
> DOMINO: That's right! Jealous of the smiles, the kind words, the tender looks to which my role entitles me.
> CRÉMONE: Jealous of you? Of you?
> DOMINO: Perhaps not of me, if you like. But of the man I appear to be. You're missing your past. . . .[6]

Achard handles the difficult personality transition artistically. The entire tone of *Domino*—not only its central precept —is strongly reminiscent of *Il Piacere dell'onestà*, the first of Pirandello's plays to be performed in France. Achard had seen it, and he writes that it "struck like a bolt of lightning."[7] That *Domino* is a unique play of considerable merit, despite this great similarity, is borne out by its inclusion, very recently, in the repertory of the Comédie Française. Its originality rests in Achard's ability to create a memorable character. As was true of Clo-Clo in *Jean de la Lune,* Domino is a theatrical creation who takes hold of the spectator. His self-assurance, his innate virtue concealed under a roguish exterior, his humor make this *his* play. Although not a dreamer, he is, nevertheless, outside the main current of life, and he is able to change the course of that current. The light touch employed in creating him is Achard's trademark. Never in his serious dramas did Pirandello have that lightness. Baldovino certainly does not show it, and only in the person of Liolà do we find a similar spirit in the Italian's works.

Marcel Achard's debt to Pirandello is most noticeable in *Le Corsaire.* This play moves on various levels of reality, dwells on the interplay between art (the cinema) and life, and dramatizes the process of personality transfer. Aspects of all plays of the trilogy of the theater-within-the-theater are synthesized in it.

In his review, shortly after Pirandello's death, André Antoine writes:

> In his recent work we find a Pirandellian influence, proving that the great Italian author has not yet completely disappeared. . . . As in works of the same nature, the characters of *Le Corsaire* are double and evolve in an original tale, touching on a problem which several others are investigating at the present time with an ardent curiosity.[8]

Like the plays of the trilogy, *Le Corsaire* has very little plot. A famous pirate, Kid Jackson, falls in love with his beautiful prisoner, Evangeline, and wins her love. Caught and condemned, he fulfills her wish that she be killed before he goes off to be hanged. But, in conformity with its Pirandellian ancestors, this tale is not told in a traditional, straightforward manner. Benjamin W. Ley's Hollywood movie studio wants to film the story. Georgia Swanee and Frank O'Hara, noted screen personalities, are engaged for the leading roles. As the producer outlines the plot, the scene shifts to the eighteenth century, and we see Kid Jackson and his Evangeline live it.

Back in Hollywood, Georgia reports that she has dreamed the entire story, down to the last detail, recurrently for ten years. As the filming progresses, the stars really fall in love. They feel that their roles are running away with them ("I have the feeling that my character is disobeying me," says Frank),[9] not only because of this new-found love, but also because they begin to feel uneasy about passages in the script. As they are about to rehearse the pirate's killing of Evangeline, Frank explains that "as soon as we arrive at this passage, I have the feeling that she is really going to die." [10] And in fact, after the make-believe stabbing, Georgia faints. This is the same device used in the double death of the children and in the fainting of the actress playing Mommina at the conclusion of *Sei personaggi in cerca d'autore* and *Questa sera si recita a soggetto,* respectively.

This technique is also employed by Achard in the last scene, in which the entire company has moved to a pirate ship in the Caribbean for authenticity in filming the hanging scene. The love Frank and Georgia have for each other has now become tinged with ominous overtones of the love between Kid Jackson and Evangeline. It is thus significant that Georgia's act of tossing overboard a scarf that had actually belonged to the historical Evangeline—a symbolic act by which the actress emphasizes the end of the character's influence over her—is immediately followed by an accident in the hanging scene that almost costs O'Hara his life. Only at the end does the couple succeed (or at least this is the impression given) in casting off the spell of their roles: their only memento now is the devotion of the pirate and his Evangeline, which has reached out to become their own.

O'Hara and Georgia Swanee become as fully immersed in and captured by their roles as Hinkfuss' troupe. Gradually, the personalities of the eighteenth-century characters are trans-

ferred to their own, and the emotions of the scenario are felt
by its interpreters. This bridges the constant interplay between
the reality of the movie company and the illusion of their
film and is comparable to the levels of action in *Ciascuno a
suo modo*—the play on "stage" and the happenings in the
"lobby." In *Le Corsaire*, there are the further levels of
Georgia's dream premonitions and of actors rehearsing a scene
just lived by "real" people. This latter device is the same
one seen in *Sei personaggi*, and in both plays the actors cannot do justice to life.

Using Pirandello's methods, Achard finds what the Sicilian
made clear in the trilogy: art is fixed while life changes and,
when the two come in contact, they tend to interfere with one
another. "It is a great spectacle and it is an entrancing spectacle," writes Fortunat Strowski with considerable justification
in *Paris-Midi*. But it is incomprehensible how as serious a
critic as Strowski can go on to say: "It is the most original that
has been seen since Pirandello's *Six Characters*." [11] Despite
its indisputable virtues, *Le Corsaire*'s strongest point is not its
originality. Basically it is Pirandello—even if of the Achard
variety—and thus his statement is overenthusiastic. This is not
to belittle an admirable play, but Strowski passes over great
and highly original plays that were produced in Paris in the
years between 1923 and 1938.

No part of Achard's theater is likely to be considered the
most original of its time, for it is too solidly a part of its heritage. What he did, he did extremely well, but he created his
plays out of familiar material. Many of the world's best dramatists have done the same, but they are not the ones to be
credited with the most originality. In fact, Achard's claim to
fame lies in the ability to bestow his particular touch on
unspectacular plays, which in another's hands might become

trivial, but which in his form an important part of the French theater of the thirties.

Armand Salacrou's theater is modern because it punctuates the absurdity of contemporary life, its illusory aspect, its corruption. In plays that have spanned some thirty years, Salacrou has commented on many degenerate phases of our age: totalitarianism and the public promulgation of ignorance, the excesses of advertising, the betrayal of friends under the duress of enemy occupation, the sham of the movie industry. He is classified among the writers of the decade now under consideration because that was his most important period of productivity and because the absurdity that underlies his plays is not the philosophic absurdity of the Existentialists, which has dominated the postwar theater, but one based on the common-sense observations of a playwright. Salacrou's theater changes in mood and form with the years. Underlying most of it, sometimes noticeably, sometimes faintly, is the influence of Pirandello.

Pont de l'Europe (1927), an early play confused by hazy surrealism, abounds in Pirandellian concepts and dialogue. There is an element at once mysterious and corrupt in the small, middle-European kingdom which, according to prophecy, agrees to accept as king and omnipotent ruler a man who will appear in the country, walking through the dust on the road. It is amusing that this man turns out to be a young former student from the Latin Quarter, but it is also a bitter comment on the thin thread of fate by which nations can be led. Jérôme, the Frenchman, marries the late king's daughter and rules until a revolution, in which his queen and son are killed, forces him to flee back to France, leaving the country prey to an uncertain future once again.

Into this tenuous frame is brought—quite gratuitously—a company of French actors, including an actress and a dancer, both of whom had formerly been Jérôme's mistresses, to stage a play that the new king has written about his past. Performed without an audience, the play becomes intermingled with actual conversations between the actors. Since they are the ones about whom the drama was written, and since Jérôme plays himself, the shifts from stage to reality occur so imperceptibly that it is difficult to tell them apart. As in *Sei personaggi* and in *Ciascuno a suo modo,* the characters exist on the twin levels of their own existence and of their theatrical portrayal of themselves. As in those two works and in *Questa sera si recita a soggetto,* the play-within-the-play reaches out to affect the reality of the play; one of the actors who loves one of the actresses hangs himself upon learning from their performance that she loves Jérôme. "Why he is hanged. He is really hanged! Help," cries the Assistant Prefect, on realizing that this is no make-believe.[12] This death underlines the reality of the king's script and answers his question to the actors: "Can one really LIVE one's role one day?"[13] One cannot only live one's role, one can die in it.

There are further instances of Pirandellism. As the play is being enacted, a stagehand accidentally lets fall a backdrop depicting Paris, and, ignoring their scripts, the actors begin to reminisce about their lives in that city. At another point, when they finish a part of the prepared text, they continue speaking impromptu because they have already lived their roles. Elsewhere a higher level of reality is suggested by bringing the audience into the story:

THE MINISTER: You are not going to betray us at least, are you?

THE KEEPER: Oh! (*He points to the public*) What would all these people who are listening to us think of me?

THE ASSISTANT PREFECT *aghast*: Someone is listening to us?
Let's speak lower. . . .[14]

The king, himself, expresses one of Pirandello's favorite ideas:
"But the reality of appearance is already a reality, after all." [15]
There is much in *Le Pont de l'Europe* to make one think
of the Italian playwright. But the play lacks unity and clarity,
and it reveals that Salacrou's artistry is still insecure. Most
important of all, and despite the stress on the nature of reality,
none of its characters is real enough to come alive in the mind
of the audience. Salacrou's successes in later years are written
in a different style, more direct and less symbolic than his early
failures. But even this early play reflects the nihilism of Salacrou's major work. This nihilism stems from the absurdity that
he observes, unrelieved by any belief in a God. Only during
the war did Salacrou at last find a God-substitute in his country.

In *Atlas-Hotel* (1931), Salacrou finally created living characters. Its hero, Auguste, lives in his own world, removed from
reality, and he accordingly builds a hotel in the middle of the
desert. *Les Frénétiques,* first performed in 1934, extends the
world of make-believe to an entire generation. *Les Frénétiques*
are the frenzied creators of mass opiates—the moguls of the
movie industry. The author exposes the false and depraved
standards on which this industry is based, and no saving grace
relieves the blackness of the portrayal.

The following year, Salacrou produced a genuine masterpiece, *L'Inconnue d'Arras.* Ironically, the flashback technique—
a man reliving his life in the fraction of time between the
suicidal shot and death—is borrowed from that maligned world
of the cinema. Nicholas, the valet, who acts as the guide
through Ulysse's past, warns his dying master of the scenes
that are about to be seen with words that echo the Father in
Sei personaggi: "What has been will be repeated. How terrible

the scene is going to be." [16] For Nicholas knows that this re-enactment will be only another disillusionment.

Ulysse's wife, the cause of the tragedy because she has betrayed him with his best friend, tries to justify herself. Her betrayal was insignificant compared to her love for him. "I loved you for three years, except for these last three days," says Yolande. "Why would three days carry more weight than three years?" [17] This was the essence of the Father's defense against the Step-Daughter's accusation.

Ulysse's last hope for finding a meaning in the life that is ebbing rests with the unknown girl he had met in Arras years earlier. But this hope, too, is shattered because she represents herself to him only as he has romanticized her, the product of his imagination. Because she had never kept the appointment they had made, her real nature remains hidden from him.

Only mediocrity is left as Ulysse prepares to shoot himself again—in the re-creation of the scene. As time runs out, cognizant of the absurdity of life, he realizes that personal salvation consists in recognizing and accepting the mediocrity of the human condition. His life had been "[a] complex woven of the grotesque and the tragic, of dreams and of realities." [18] In death he is alone and abandoned, "naked," like Ersilia Drei. The air he wanted to breathe was too rarefied for life.

La Terre est ronde (1938) is a good play but somewhat too complicated to be successful. In Savonarola and fifteenth-century Florence Salacrou finds a fitting simile for Hitler and Europe's anguish in the late 1930's. The proposition that the earth is round—a theory that the Florentine ruler tried to suppress as false and illusory—serves as the symbol of the ideas that struggle against despotism, the illusions of one day which must become the realities of the next.

La Marguerite (1944) bears a strong resemblance to *La Vita che ti diedi*. A father refuses to believe that his son died in a shipwreck, and the illusion that he survived materializes in the person of a passing railwayman whom the blind father takes for his son. The young man lends himself to this deception long enough for the old man to die happily. Marguerite, the son's widow, is inspired by her father-in-law's faith against all odds, leaving the man who had become her lover to wait for the husband who will never return. The old man's tenacity in preserving his illusion has restored some sort of reality to his son. The mother of the Italian play never succeeded in this, but her efforts were directed along the same path. Salacrou's disenchantment with life suddenly comes to the forefront at the end as chaos invades a touching story. We learn that the son had been a drunkard, the father a chaser of women, and Marguerite and her lover the most mediocre of people. The absurdity of the entire situation becomes apparent because the characters for whom Salacrou had elicited our sympathy are not worthy of it. The mood continues to be bleak.

Friendship, patriotism, and pity for the dead and the survivors of the Resistance tempers the blackness in *Les Nuits de la colère* (1946), a sober, well-constructed examination of France under occupation. But by the following year, Salacrou is back satirizing society once again. In *L'Archipel Lenoir* (1947), he indicts the great industrialists of the era and expresses his profound indignation at the behavior of the monied circles.

The great liqueur manufacturing family Lenoir is depicted as a vicious group of beasts of prey. They are set into diabolical motion by a ludicrous situation: scandal threatens because the elderly grandfather had seduced a young girl whose father is bringing charges. Not only would jail mean scandal for the entire family; it would also cause a slump in the sale of Lenoir liqueurs. The grandfather's loving family discovers one way out—the old man must commit suicide before his arrest. But

Paul-Albert Lenoir is thoroughly unreasonable. He is only seventy-three years old and he still wants to live. His son-in-law, Adolphe, is therefore chosen by the family to shoot Lenoir—an unusual sort of mercy killing. But in the far recess of his soul Adolphe finds a touch of humanity and hands the gun to his father-in-law so that he may shoot himself honorably. The grandfather still has not resigned himself to death, and he shoots Adolphe instead, wounding him in his arm. When all seems lost, the valet saves the day: for one million francs and the Lenoir sales management in Mexico, he will marry the wronged girl and make her deny the accusation against the grandfather.

The play thus ends "happily." Its caricature of the Lenoir family is so gross that it is always amusing. But behind it looms a bitter cynicism that reveals only disgust with society rather than real humor. Salacrou, who had shown the need for illusions previously, decries them when they harm someone. Pirandello had made the same point in *Il Giuoco delle parti* and in other plays. To sacrifice an old man on the altar of respectability and high sales in order to create a public illusion about a private reality is a travesty of human behavior.

The last Salacrou play to be considered is *Poof* (1950), a *comédie-ballet*. This delightful farce is a spoof of the professional illusionists: the members of the advertising field. Until he realizes the essential truth that is at the basis of all advertising—that human beings are stupid and need someone to tell them what is good and what is bad, what is real and what is not—until that moment, Poof is even unable to distribute free leaflets successfully. But with his new knowledge he soars to Olympian heights. Soon he becomes an advertising czar—the prime mover of all business. His slogans have made him the taste-maker of the entire country and his unchallenged position as supreme illusion-creator inspires him to initiate the greatest of all advertising projects: he will give people the illusion that they are happy. "Why didn't God think of it. After so much effort to create the world, it would have been so easy for him to create the illusion of happiness on earth." [19] Poof will attend to what God neglected. If people can be sold on a product, they can be sold on happiness. All that matters is to make them think they are happy. "I can already see a beautiful poster . . . soft colors . . . Another one . . . a glimmer of sunshine . . . 'Be happy.' And all men will have left to do will be to breathe! That's the only thing I cannot do for them." [20]

The last obstacle facing Poof is a group formed to kill him in order to break the stranglehold of advertising. But he has little difficulty in winning them to his side: he will personally direct a gigantic campaign against all advertising. And as the play ends, Poof reigns supreme.

Behind this farcical satire, there is no sardonic stress as in *L'Archipel Lenoir*. Salacrou is not indignant at the excesses in advertising, and the prevailing mood remains strictly humorous.

Pirandello's ideas and techniques are seen throughout a good part of Salacrou's theater, either in the foreground or in the background. Silvio d'Amico refers to "the obvious Pirandellism of Armand Salacrou's most highly colored repertoire." [21] Almost everywhere in the French writer's theater is there emphasis on the chimerical aspect of existence, and Salacrou treats the role of illusions in life from as many points of view as did Pirandello.

Salacrou also shares Pirandello's pessimism. Both are struck by the chaos of the modern world and of the individual in it. The Italian described it more in the human personality, the Frenchman in our institutions, but they agree on the absurd condition of man, on the moral degeneration that has taken place. Of the two, Salacrou is probably the more disillusioned because only rarely can he find the compassion for suffering mankind that Pirandello feels strongly.

Armand Salacrou's theater is essentially modern because it portrays the anguish of a generation. Like his generation, he can never find the God he so desperately seeks. He searches for a meaning in life, and uncovers only absurdity—an absurdity of life that is unredeemed even by the liberty of action of the Existentialists. The rigid determinism that he postulates removes any hope that might remain. Salacrou's theater is the concise expression of his *Weltanschauung*, which together with his skillful dramatic expression unquestionably makes him one of the leading contemporary French playwrights.

The most highly individualistic of all modern French playwrights is undoubtedly Jean Giraudoux. His theater bears a personal stamp so completely his own that the French critics, to describe that quality, had to invent the adjective *giralducien*. His great individuality naturally causes the critic to pause before discussing influences.

If the great Limousin is included in this book, it is not with the intent of proving him to be a Pirandellian disciple. Yet Giraudoux must be mentioned here because some of the ideas we have found to be Pirandello's reappear in his works. They are by no means dominant in Giraudoux, and the possibility of conscious adaptation of the Italian's theories is somewhat problematical. Either Giraudoux was directly influenced to some degree by Pirandello's plays, or, as seems more probable, he reflected the theatrical atmosphere of his time. It is not of primary importance—nor can it be shown conclusively—which of these theories is true. What matters more is that in Giraudoux's theater can be found reflections of the ideas which Pirandello had sown in the French theater in the 1920's and 1930's.

Of the themes discussed in Chapter II, the need for illusions is the one most emphasized by Giraudoux. If the atmosphere of *Intermezzo* (1933) is typically *giralducienne* in its delicate magic, it does, basically, deal with people's need for illusions. Isabelle is brought close to death by the intolerance of the "dream killer," the Inspector, that representative of nineteenth-century materialism, who will not allow fantasy to exist. His purpose is to destroy the specter that had been reported in the neighborhood, but his method threatens Isabelle who fondly believes in its existence. Juxtaposed to the Inspector are the druggist and the controller who, through love and common sense, find the proper solution. They understand the girl's fantasy and have a remedy for it, whereas the Inspector has none. Illusions, Giraudoux points out, should never be ruthlessly destroyed—understanding and love alone can adapt them to normal, everyday life.

Illusion is the thing in *L'Apollon de Bellac* (1942) also. This charming one act farce demonstrates the use of extreme flattery. The gentleman of the play tells the girl who is seeking a job that, in order to get ahead, all she need do is tell all men that they are handsome, that, in fact, they remind her of the nonexistent Apollo of Bellac. The scheme has the most gratifying results: she soon has everyone at her feet, while all the men are deliriously happy.

Most important, however, is the posthumous *La Folle de Chaillot* (1945), a play which differs from most of Giraudoux's productions because of its social criticism. This delightful comedy offers a cure for the world's ills—simply the annihilation of all swindlers, schemers, and other undesirables. This

notable task is achieved by the madwoman of Chaillot and her
companions, as zany a group as ever populated a stage. They
live in their own little world of fancy, which seems so real
to them that it eventually imposes itself on the spectator. By
the end of the play we are much more likely to consider normal
the madness of the women, their conversations with dead or
invisible persons and animals, than the fantastic plot of the
"normal" people to turn Paris into a vast oil field.

Again it must be stressed that the mood of this Giraudoux
play differs sharply from Pirandello. And yet parts of the
dialogue are strongly reminiscent of the Italian. The President,
for instance, referring to his varied activities in life, says: ". . .
all I have had to do was to give myself over to each of these
lifeless masks. . . ." [22] The conception of the personality as
mask is one we have observed previously. Both the charm with
which Giraudoux has infused this play and the Pirandellian
view of the strength of illusion are brought out in two speeches
by Aurélie in Act II about the invisible dead dog, Dicky.

> You know he [Dicky] is welcome here. We do our best to
> receive him and to treat him as well as when he was alive.
> This is a memory which has taken on a peculiar form in your
> mind. We respect it.

> You know just as well as I do that this poor little Dicky
> is a touching convention between us, but still only a conven-
> tion. And besides, you are the one who is making it impos-
> sible. When you went to your niece's house last month and
> left him with me, we got along perfectly. He doesn't bark.
> He doesn't eat. But when you are here, he is all one hears
> about. I will not take him on my lap for anything in the
> world. [23]

Belief in Dicky has kept him alive even after his death and
the madwomen accept him, knowing all the while that he no
longer exists. Could not one make a comparison to *La Vita*

che ti diedi, although the one is in the realm of folly and the other concerns basic human suffering?

Giraudoux merely touches upon Pirandello's concept of the theater-within-the-theater. To be sure, the Frenchman did not have to go beyond the Alps to find inspiration for *L'Impromptu de Paris* (1937); it is clearly modeled after Molière's *L'Impromptu de Versailles.* In fact, that is the play which the Jouvet company is rehearsing as M. Robineau, the Deputy charged with drafting a bill on the theater, enters. To portray what the theater is, Pirandello would have had his characters show us; Giraudoux makes them talk about it. Nevertheless, the very fact that he uses this method at all is interesting. In their defense of the theater, Jouvet and his players extol the superior reality of their art over life: "the theater consists of being real in the unreal." [24]

Maxime Chastaing considers that Giraudoux's creations are characters in search of themselves, in the best Pirandellian tradition of dual personality:

> Two Forestiers in one man: *Siegfried et le Limousin.* Two Isabelles in one: *Intermezzo.* Two Hanses: *Ondine.* Two husbands for Alcmena: the real one who appears false to her, and the false one who appears real to her: *Amphytrion 38.* Giraudoux's creatures change when they come in contact with others, and they lose themselves in the various qualities others attribute to them, like actors in different roles. They are in search of themselves. [25]

It is probably far-fetched to think of two Isabelles and two Hanses. Although Isabelle believes in the specter, it does not require a separate personality for her to teach school, nor does Hans's infidelity after his wedding to Ondine testify to anything but this stupidity. Nor is Alcmène's personality multiple. Indeed she is one of the most singleminded of Giraudoux's characters, the same model of marital stability and good sense with her husband and with Jupiter disguised as Amphytrion. But Forestier certainly is a dual character in the Pirandellian sense of the word.

Four plays resemble each other markedly in their use of the theme of amnesia leading to multiple personality: Giraudoux's *Siegfried* in 1928; Jean Sarment's *Le Pêcheur d'ombres* and Pirandello's *Enrico IV* in the 1920's; and Anouilh's *Le Voyageur sans bagage* in 1937. Sarment's play and Giraudoux's prototype for his (the novel, *Siegfried et le Limousin*) were written before *Enrico IV* was performed in France, eliminating any possibility of influence. The Italian tragedy and the resounding success it had in Paris probably prompted Giraudoux to refashion his novel into the play, *Siegfried*. Gabriel Marcel also detects the Italian's imprint on this play:

> Pirandello's importance for contemporary French dramatists is undeniable. . . . I am thinking of a play like *Le Voyageur sans bagage,* for instance, which seems very Pirandellian. But between the two there was *Siegfried,* and it does not seem certain to me that Giraudoux himself was not influenced by Pirandello.[26]

It is obvious, of course, that Giraudoux's principal purpose is not that of the other three plays—to study the facets of a multiple personality. *Siegfried* deals, in particular, with Franco-German relations and, by extension, with the basic similarities and slight differences between all people. The amnesiac who has a new personality after his illness is the ideal vehicle for this subject.

Forestier-Siegfried has two distinct personalities. As Forestier, he is typically French—gentle and mild-mannered, a young writer who was reported missing in the war; as Siegfried, he becomes the epitome of good things German—sober and efficient, the respected, admired leader of the "new Germany." If Jacques, after learning the truth about himself, returns to France to resume his original life, his decision emphasizes that one's nationality *does* have some import.* If the difference in his personalities is due merely to a process of education and re-education, it proves that those traits generally considered to be national characteristics are, in fact, not characteristics at all but rather products of national education. One need not become excessively technical and argue that education itself is a reflection of national characteristics; Giraudoux's basic plea for peace based on understanding among peoples is valuable nonetheless.

Giraudoux's ideals, his poetic style and imagination, his wit and his fancifulness mark him as a dramatist far removed from Pirandello. The combination of these qualities, together with his solid sense of dramatic structure and his gift for creating brilliant dialogue, place him at the head of the gifted group of French dramatists in the period between the two World Wars. He does not belong among the Pirandellians any more than he belongs to any other category except *giralducien*. But he has brought into his theater some of the ideas with which the Italian enriched the French stage, adapting each one to suit his own temperament and dramatic theories. The fact that these ideas are found even in the most original playwright of the times attests to the great impression Pirandello made on his Gallic contemporaries.

Fernand Crommelynck's theater was strongly colored by Pirandello's. The author of *Le Cocu magnifique* was sufficiently drawn to the Sicilian to translate his *Come prima, meglio di prima* for its production at the Théâtre de Grenelle in March, 1928, as *Comme avant, mieux qu'avant*. His own

---

* By returning to France, Jacques accepts his past, which is precisely what Gaston, Enrico, and Jean, in the three similar plays, are each in his own way unable or unwilling to do.

work reflects not the outwardly brilliant Pirandellian techniques but the inner stress and tragedy of Pirandellian characters, buffeted about in a world of uncertain values. Eric Bentley
links him with Anouilh as a disciple of the Italian:

> Crommelynck . . . is distinctly Pirandellian in his work;
> and from Crommelynck to Anouilh is but a step. While
> Lenormand, in such a play as *Le Crépuscule du théâtre,*
> takes over easily separable technical features of *Six Charac-
> ters,* Crommelynck and Anouilh are Pirandellian in a deeper
> sense: they share his metaphysical anguish and, like him, they
> express it in a passionate version of erotic relations.[27]

Chaud et froid (1935) is representative of Crommelynck's
affinity to Pirandello because it incorporates several of the
Italian's themes. It concerns the sudden death of a man, Dom,
whose wife, Léona, had been betraying him with a series of
lovers. Dom had always been considered a dullard and a boor,
and it is with great surprise, therefore, that Léona sees the
arrival of the woman who had been his mistress for the last ten
years—Félie, with whom Dom had been romantic and charming. He had actually been two totally different people in two
aspects of his life.

Unconcerned about her infidelities while her husband was
alive, Léona becomes captivated by her role of widow and
puts an end to her affairs. Like Baldovino, she is intoxicated
by *la volupté de l'honneur* and at last is a true wife. Léona
even becomes jealous of Félie, who wants to commit suicide
in her grief. This act would challenge her newly-adopted
position as wife, and Léona, by ordering her last lover to
seduce Félie, "relieves" her of her grief for Dom. Now Dom,
in death, belongs exclusively to his widow, who has assimilated
Félie's role and who even believes that her husband and she
had loved one another.

The principal action is precipitated by the maid's report

that Dom, before dying, revealed that he had an idea. Everyone begins to speculate about what the idea might have been.
It is believed that it concerned ideal marriage conditions, but
this is never clarified. The essential thing is that the Idea (it
is now capitalized) spreads throughout the country, as expounded by "Domists." The adherents of "Domism" are
divided into two main schools of thought, whose symbols—
the chameleon and the hourglass—stress their emphasis on
change and constancy, respectively. Dom's room will become a
sanctuary, and, in the final triumph, the two opposing fac-
tions unite for the greater glory of "Domism." The idea cannot be stopped—even when the maid reveals that she had
invented the story of Dom's idea.

The Pirandellian concepts are clearly delineated. Dom, as
he appears to his wife and to his mistress, suggests a case of
multiple personality, for he is different with each of the two
women. The dominant theme is that of illusions. One instance
is Léona's increasing conviction that she and Dom had enjoyed
a genuine husband-wife relationship. By the end of the play
this illusion is promoted to full reality for her.

The development and propagation of Domism is, of course,
a clear case of an illusion imposing itself. That there never
was an idea is only an incidental irony. The essential point
is that an idea nobody knew becomes equivalent to a religion.
It is a clever satire of an age dominated by misunderstood
"isms" and of the modern theory of propaganda that the
bigger the lie, the more easily accepted by the people.

Crommelynck displays a thorough mastery of the Pirandellian repertory. *Chaud et froid* is imbued with the same
farcical humor found in the Italian's theater, and the ideas are
skillfully interwoven. Even the title reminds us of the Italian's,
although it is more enigmatic than descriptive. The Belgian's
debt to Pirandello is clear-cut in this play.

For fifty years, Sacha Guitry wrote plays with himself as principal subject. It would be easy to give in to the temptation of dismissing him as unworthy of mention in a serious study, but it is hard to deny the compelling attraction he had for audiences of an entire half century. Perhaps this is attributable to the fascination a gigantic ego holds for people. But Guitry was more than a simple exhibitionist. He had a keen sense of the dramatic and a sharp humorous verve that thrived on misunderstandings and mistaken identity. What he lacked was substance behind the shiny exterior—and a main character who was not always Guitry.

Sacha Guitry was the kind of playwright who could recognize a good thing when he saw it. And so, he too went through a phase of Pirandellism. "Lately, M. Sacha Guitry has taken hold of the Pirandellian prism," wrote Paul Werrie,[28] and *Florence, L'École du mensonge,* and *Quand jouons-nous la comédie!* illustrate this phase. An examination of the last of these plays is sufficient to point out his imitation of the Italian.

Quand jouons-nous la comédie! (1935) follows the now familiar pattern of the play-within-the-play. The only difference between Pirandello's use of this technique and Guitry's —a revealing difference—is that the French writer uses it as a simple hoax perpetrated on the audience. Guitry wastes its effect by not revealing until the surprise ending that the main part of the play is itself a play.

In the Prologue, Elle and Lui, a famous operatic couple, discuss in whispers during a performance their plan to retire. They decide they will not make any formal announcement, because in that way their admirers will simply think that they are singing elsewhere and their memory will stay alive. Elle and Lui do not realize, however, that the opera is being broadcast and that their asides are being diffused by the microphones. When this is revealed to them, their decision becomes irrevocable, since the entire country now knows of it. They explain that they want to abandon the opera at the peak of their careers and not wait until their artistry deteriorates. As the lengthy Prologue ends, their dramatist-friend declares that he will write a play about them, in which he wants them to star.

The spectator cannot help but feel that the three acts which follow are a simple continuation of the story. Although the dramatist had announced a play about the couple, it was to deal with their success and their dramatic retirement, whereas the plot of these acts concerns their rift after retiring. Constance (Elle) and Bernard (Lui) find that their proverbially great love has vanished with advancing years. They have nourished their relationship only with passion, never allowing it to develop into the tenderness needed in later years. Resentment, suspicion, and jealousy of their past are the remnants of their former idyll. But despite their failure as husband and wife, they choose to stay together because neither can imagine living with someone else and because they cannot bear to shatter the illusions which others have about them.

The brief Epilogue shifts backstage, revealing that the three acts had really been the drama written by the friend of the singers-turned-actors. It is a trick, and a foolish one at that. Guitry did not need it to portray his situation. This gratuitous use of a Pirandellian technique is of the sort that was decried by critics and caused the temporary decline of Pirandello's reputation. Colette pointed out the superficiality of the play:

> The name of Pirandello has been spoken and printed with reference to *Quand jouons-nous la comédie!* A superficial glance may link two types of dramatists so differently gifted, but one recognizes at once that the author of the new comedy at the Théâtre de Paris—a clear mind in the French tradition —wanted only to write a trap play.[29]

The play is, in fact, a trap to catch the audience. The Pirandellism of the play-within-the-play and of the illusions of a fond public preserving a marriage is purely external. Behind the façade there is nothing. Sacha Guitry was beyond his element of the Boulevards when he tried to incorporate the cerebral quality of the Italian's theater into his own realm of flighty sentimental comedy.

Jean Cocteau's versatility is proverbial. Practically every type of written artistic expression has been employed by him at one time or another—from novels to theater, to poetry, to the cinema, to stories for ballet and a libretto for an opera, plus criticism of various sorts. In his theatrical production itself, Cocteau has displayed considerable versatility: he has written romantic dramas, half-modernized versions of Greek classics, bourgeois drama, and tales of magic and enchantment. A man of such varied interests was quite naturally interested in Pirandello.

Francis Fergusson detects Pirandello's influence in *La Machine infernale* (1934): "*The Infernal Machine* uses the Pirandellesque stage: *i.e.,* the stage as an art-medium like that of the painter or musician; the stage as Pirandello's characters use it, to present a brilliant and final image of their tragedies." [30] Cocteau accepts the stage itself as a creative medium, as Pirandello accepted it. By not forcing it to be merely a backdrop and a scene of action, he enables the stage to become an active participant in the play, an additional dimension. Thus, Cocteau takes the audience into his confidence by presenting his modern Oedipus against the background of the Oedipus myth. He dispenses with the customary exposition because everyone knows it, freeing himself for his real purpose—the emphasis of the aspects that will make this *Cocteau's* Oedipus.

The title stresses the author's view of the destiny of man. No longer are men the prey of a dispassionate and blind fatality. Cocteau portrays them as victimized by a malign, ruthless doom. By conceiving it not only as a machine, as did the Greeks, but as an infernal one, he expresses fate in the only terms a writer of the thirties could—as a function of the absurdity of life.

Of course, the ultimate disclosure of Oedipus' past is a supreme example of the tragic confrontation of the maskless self before the mirror of truth. Oedipus' self-mutilation is the prototype of all the audible inward cries of agony that follow.

Les Chevaliers de la Table Ronde (1937) also takes up a myth. In telling the stories of King Arthur's jealous act of killing Lancelot and Guinevere, and of Galahad's quest for the Holy Grail, Cocteau adheres to the principal lines of the legend. His inventiveness lies in the invisible character, Ginifer, Merlin's young servant, who is seen in impersonations of members of the court but never as himself. It is a novel concept for depicting personality. Ginifer's treachery and cowardliness materialize slowly in the contrast between the characters themselves and the characters while he is "in their skins," as it were.

These double identities strain the spectator's understanding of what is real and what is fake. Lancelot exclaims in confusion: "I think it is becoming difficult here to know what is reality or dream." [31] For, with his tricks and deceptions, Ginifer has cast a spell of illusions broken only by Galahad's shining vision of the superior truth that is the Grail.

Cocteau does not indulge in the facile Pirandellian imitations of a Guitry. He uses the Italian's themes sparsely but soberly, fully aware of his contribution. "It is to the degree that Pirandello focused on an inevitable problem of the theater," wrote Cocteau, "that he seems to have influenced those who, like himself, know precisely what dose of realism and of mystery the theater requires." [32] Both in *La Machine infernale* and in *Les Chevaliers de la Table Ronde,* Cocteau carefully blends the real and the illusory in a mixture that traces back to Pirandello.

It is, perhaps, no mere coincidence that the man who is considered France's leading playwright today is also the playwright who reflects most clearly the influence of Pirandello. In its themes, its treatment, and its general atmosphere, the theater of Jean Anouilh is the most Pirandellian in France. He is considered in this chapter rather than with the most recent playwrights because, generally speaking, his later plays restate the themes of his earlier ones, because he had produced a sizable number of important plays by the end of the war, and because he does not share the Existentialist absurdity endorsed by most younger dramatists. (These reasons hold true for Salacrou and Achard as well.)

Anouilh's characters, like Pirandello's, are engaged in the search for escape from life's sordidness, and they too usually choose irreality as the solution to their problems. Whereas Pirandello's plays resemble one another to the extent that they are sometimes thought of as variations on a theme, Anouilh's do not follow a master pattern. We therefore find Pirandello's influence on the French writer diffused and uneven, more pronounced in some plays and less in others. The division into *pièces noires, roses, brillantes,* and *grinçantes* underlines the varying moods in which they are written. Actually, the categories themselves are rather loose, and each one includes plays that differ radically from one another. Pirandello's influence transcends the four groups, but one must seek it in individual plays rather than in entire groups, for it is not present everywhere.

One of the Sicilian's themes recurring most markedly in the Frenchman's theater is multiplicity of personality. In the pattern of *Enrico IV*, *Siegfried*, and *Le Pêcheur d'ombres*, *Le Voyageur sans bagage* (1937) is the story of a man without a present, reaching the point of no return between his past and his future.

Amnesia is the convenient vehicle for creating this unusual situation wherein the multiplicity of a man's personality can be ideally studied, for, in his recovery, the hero, Gaston, reaches precisely that moment in his life when his past unfolds in direct opposition to his new self, revealing the painful dichotomy between the two aspects of his mind. Gaston is as different from the young Jacques who disappeared in the war as it is possible for two people to be—and yet they are the same person. By admitting that he is Jacques, Gaston would have to accept the horrid past that his former self had left behind— a past that is unbelievable in view of his gentle nature as a grown man. Therefore he reaches the difficult decision of renouncing his family and a part of himself in order to be true to himself as he now is.

Like Enrico IV, Gaston-Jacques has two totally distinct personalities, and in both cases the split occurred as a result of amnesia. Anouilh's basic conception of his hero is wholly Pirandellian. Yet Enrico becomes a tragic figure who is defeated, whereas Gaston sheds his past in a fairly satisfactory resolution of his conflict by accepting his new role as the little English boy's nephew. The character of Enrico brings up the question of insanity, and his difficulty lies in accepting the outside world. For Gaston, neither madness nor the outside world are problems. It is himself he cannot accept. "I had become used to myself," says Gaston, "I knew myself well, and suddenly here I am having to leave myself, to find another me, and to put him on like an old vest." [33] He is, to use the

Pirandellian frame of reference, a character in search of himself, a man longing for a past, yet having the most unusual liberty of being able to choose it. Anouilh expresses it with his characteristic irony:

> GASTON: It obviously frightened people that a man can live without a past. People are even wary of foundlings . . . But a man, a fully grown man, who hardly had a country, no home town, no traditions, no name . . . Blazes! What a scandal! [34]

This liberty is precious to Gaston, and he is not willing to surrender it for the past of a man who had cheated, stolen, lied, crippled his best friend, and stolen his brother's wife. Valentine, like an Existentialist, tells him: "Listen, Jacques, after all, you must accept yourself. When you get right down to it, our whole life with our fine morality and our fine liberty consists of accepting ourselves as we are." [35]

Valentine does not understand that liberty does not mean accepting what one was but what one is. For Gaston to accept what he is, he must, perforce, deny Jacques. He goes into the future without the burdensome baggage of his past in a supreme affirmation of his freedom, whereas Enrico's act of violence—it too a free act—shackles him forever in his world of fiction.

We have noted (in Chapter II) that in *Signora Morli, una e due*, Pirandello has confused a double personality with multiple facets of a single personality. *Colombe* (1951) is the treatment of a basically similar situation. Anouilh does not, however, commit the Italian's error; instead he leaves it to his hero, Julien, to think that there are two separate people called Colombe—the innocent, childlike girl he had married, and the worldly wise actress she becomes. "I forbid you . . ." he tells Colombe, referring to the wife he knew before his army service, "I forbid you to besmirch that one." [36] He can explain the drastic change only by imagining a dual Colombe, when in fact, her life in Paris was merely the catalyst that enabled the carefree facet of her personality to emerge dominant.

Another phase of the personality puzzle is given in *La Sauvage* (1934) and *Antigone* (1942). Here reappears the mask motif—people (women, as is usual in Pirandello also) who appear to the world in two contradictory manners. For Thérèse, a mediocre violinist with a shady past and a sordid background, marriage to the kind and wealthy Florent offers the unique opportunity of escape from the baseness of life. Yet, despite her longing for respectability, she deliberately plunges back into the mire of her former existence. The mask will not adhere to the face that hides behind it, and when it is torn away, Thérèse's personality conflict is resolved through the victory of her baser self.

Antigone is similarly torn in two opposing directions— her instinctive love of life is contrasted with her unrelenting drive for justice, even though the latter necessarily involves her death and the destruction of her city. Like Ersilia Drei and like Thérèse, Antigone is bent on self-destruction, and in her case also, the mask of participation in life is not solid enough to ward off her basic nihilism. She epitomizes what Anouilh has succeeded in capturing so well in the heroines of his *pièces noires*—the tragic flaw. But the flaw is not a personality trait exploited by an impassionate fatality; it is inherent in the personality structure itself.

Pauvre Bitos (1956) presents an interesting variant of the multiplicity-of-personality theme. In it, a man is forced to assume a personality not his own, but one which is similar enough so that he glides easily from one to the other. André Bitos is a young public prosecutor with many enemies. His former schoolmates dislike him for the excellent grades he had received—Bitos, the poor, scholarship-supported student, who had spent all his time studying. Others hate him for his methodical, ruthless prosecution of collaborators after the liberation. To get revenge, Maxime arranges a *dîner de têtes*, a gathering at which the participants disguise their heads as those of historical characters.

Bitos is asked to portray Robespierre; others come as Danton, Mirabeau, and sundry figures of the Reign of Terror. The accusations leveled at Robespierre are all too obviously double-edged, and Bitos is forced to defend both himself and his historic counterpart. The climax of the evening is the reliving of the shooting of Robespierre by the policeman Merda. The gun used is not loaded, but Bitos faints and then dreams of himself as Robespierre. The remainder of the play is taken up with the efforts of the guests to placate Bitos, and with the latter's inability to differentiate between those who are hostile to him and those who have genuine sympathy for him.

Pauvre Bitos is perhaps Anouilh's most bitter play. Its cynicism is unrelenting and unrelieved. As a result, one is too overwhelmed by so much vitriol and the spectator cannot help but breathe more easily when the final curtain rings down. The multiple personality theme is, however, very cleverly used by Anouilh. Bitos' personality blends with Robespierre's until the two become one. Robespierre's faults and qualities are Bitos', their backgrounds the same, their careers similar; and when Bitos indulges in a fantasy in which he is Robespierre, it seems perfectly natural. The whole conception of Bitos is well within the Pirandellian picture of personality.

A considerable number of Anouilh's plays involve, in some way, the problem of the relativity of truth. Most often, this relativity is brought into play in a situation which concerns the preservation of people's private worlds—an idea with which

Pirandello, like Ibsen before him, was preoccupied. But while the Norwegian's attitude showed social protest and the Italian's somber pessimism and outrage at man's stupidity, the Frenchman's work is permeated by sadness and by an irony, sometimes savage, that accompanies the conviction that happiness is, at best, very difficult to attain and that most human beings move in mutually exclusive spheres.

Both *Ardèle ou la Marguerite* (1949) and *La Valse des toréadors* (1952) deal with generals' households living in sham, and in both cases a private fiction is allowed to dominate outsiders, with damaging effects. Pirandello maintained in *Il Giuoco delle parti*, in *Liolà*, and in other plays, that a person is entitled to his private idea of himself as long as it does not hurt someone else. Anouilh provides us here with two cases in point.

The marriages in Ardèle's family are pretenses. Husbands and wives, lacking the courage to admit that they no longer love each other and concerned only with their mistresses and lovers, would rather pretend to the outside world that they are happily married couples. This, by itself, would not bring harm to anyone else, but they try to impose these artifices on Ardèle, the hunchbacked sister, who falls in love with the equally hunchbacked tutor. Confused and morally twisted itself, the family does not even recognize the importance of a true love, and, aware only that the tutor's social position makes a liaison with Ardèle unacceptable, it proceeds to break up the romance and drive the deformed couple to suicide.

The children in this play also suffer because of the examples of conjugal relationships set for them. When they play at being adults, they only fight and scream and beat each other. "You know perfectly well," the countess tells her husband, "that it is only a matter of respecting appearances, of not presenting a scandal for the world to see." [37] But she does not realize that, in building a fence of fiction around the family group, unwilling members are included who, unable to escape, perish.

General Léon Saint-Pé of *La Valse des toréadors* is guilty of the same crime. The fiction of his marriage, enduring through his wife's illness and his seduction of countless girls, is preserved not so much for appearances as out of cowardice. Without realizing that he is destroying himself and those around him, Léon refuses to end his marriage because he wants to spare his wife. As a result, the patient Ghislaine, his true love, wastes seventeen years of her life, and *la Générale* has to endure his constant infidelities. Clearly, the proper solution would have been to cut cleanly and swiftly, to avoid ensnaring innocent people in the general's fiction.

La Répétition ou l'Amour puni (1950) is one further variation of the sham marriage motif. Into the heart of an aristocratic *ménage à quatre* comes Tigre's love for Lucile, the teacher he has hired for his orphanage. This is an intolerable situation for both his wife and his mistress, not because it involves their love but because it involves their dignity: Lucile is from a much lower station in life. Their solution, to destroy the couple, succeeds with the help of the villain, Héro—a villain of very unlikely motivation.

All these are people attempting to protect, at the expense of other people, the world they have created. Their moral position is untenable, and they either fail completely or destroy themselves along with the outsiders who become entangled in their web. *L'Amour puni* is the subtitle of the last play, and it might well serve for all three, for it emphasizes the stalemate which love suffers.

Structurally, *La Répétition* differs from the other two plays in a way that is strongly reminiscent of Pirandello. Tigre and his friends are rehearsing Marivaux's *La Double Inconstance*, and the dialogue of the play-in-rehearsal blends in and becomes a part of the words spoken by the characters themselves, just as the situation in the eighteenth-century play is an echo of what is transpiring at the chateau. (The interplay is heightened by the *marivaudage* with which Anouilh endows his dialogue.) This intimate relation between a play being enacted and another, included in the first, being rehearsed, makes one think inevitably of *Sei personaggi*. Hortensia says to Tigre, as the actors might tell the Father, "If it's a game you are playing, it is not funny! You have just told us that we were not ourselves. . . ." [38]

Moreover, the characters are aware that their lives as people and as actors overlap. "I have to disgust a little," Héro explains. "It's part of my role. Not the one in Marivaux's play, but in the other one—the one I really play." [39] And later, Hortensia tells Villebosse, who is anxious for rehearsal to start: "We're already acting. Hadn't you noticed?" [40] Life, these characters feel, as does Pirandello, is composed of roles that its participants play.

A little Pirandellian touch, too, is the dropping of the curtain at the conclusion of Act II, as the group rehearses its curtain calls, bringing to mind the accidental curtain in *Sei personaggi*. Of further interest are Tigre's ideas as director for the presentation of the Marivaux comedy. He conceives the play as a direct outgrowth of life, which becomes animated in front of spectators, an idea very reminiscent of *Questa sera si recità a soggetto*. "A character gets up from the table and he calls on another, they begin to talk, people listen to them and believe they actually have something to say to each other. . . ." [41] To prepare for this, an eighteenth-century turn is to be given to the conversation, and the transition is complete: *La Double Inconstance* will emerge slowly, as a perfected illusion, out of a twentieth-century dinner party.

Y'avait un prisonnier came early in Anouilh's career (1935), but it already anticipated the later themes. Ludovic, returning from fifteen years in prison, resists his family's attempt to ensnare him in their world of business deceit, although they threaten to commit him to an insane asylum unless he espouses it. His desperate dive into the ocean to seek freedom is the symbol of every man's struggle for his own privacy and man's desperate rebellion against having to share others' secret illusions.

Illusions are needed, but they must remain personal. In prison, Ludovic was alone, craving companionship. He would think of a person and "I concentrated on the memory of him until, in some way, I created his invisible presence around me." [42] Ludovic's wife tries to foster his illusions by becoming what he wants her to be:

> Finished, the ardent, strong, magnificent woman you know; perhaps he wants a frightened woman in love, coupled with a good little housewife . . . ? From that point it was only a simple step to transform myself completely with my feminine flexibility. I took that step. Overnight . . . I became a different woman; . . . since it was not this personality which suited him, I wanted to try another one. [43]

The concept of the changing personality is here, but not on the involuntary inner level, as in Pirandello or as displayed in *Maya*. Rather it is a deliberate and basically false desire to distort oneself willfully to conform to what others would like to see.

Weakness in plot and characterization reduce the effectiveness of this play, and the general impression is one of artifice not too skillfully contrived, but *Y'avait un prisonnier* contains the germs of the later Anouilh.

In *L'Invitation au château* (1947), we find the marked contrast between the profound reality of the person of Isabelle, who is actually a sham, and the falsity of the very real characters of the play. Truth, as it concerns the validity of their existences, is again proven to be relative.

Lastly, two Anouilh plays, both *pièces roses—Le Rendez-vous de Senlis* (1937) and *Léocadia* (1939)—clearly illustrate the Pirandellian antithesis. Georges, the hero of the first-named play, belongs to the line of characters who create around themselves intricate fictions to compensate for unpleasant facts. To make up for the baseness of his parents and of his best friend, Robert, he creates new parents and a new Robert. This process takes place in his imagination at first. It is then extended to Isabelle, the girl with whom he has arranged the rendezvous in Senlis. Finally, it assumes reality through the physical presence of the "parents"—enacted by hired actors. That this use of players is only the last stage of the creative process is borne out by Georges' advice to the actors. "You must understand however that I did not send for you to have you imagine theatrical fathers or mothers at will. These characters exist. These characters are already half alive. Someone believes in them. . . ." [44] These parents, in other words, came into existence when Georges conjured them up in his imagination, and they became alive when they were impersonated in Senlis. Even Robert recognizes this in saying "appearances are more than enough to create a world." [45]

In this play, Anouilh also strays into another of Pirandello's themes—the art-life opposition. As the hired father and mother rehearse their roles with Georges, they are all carried away by their inventions until they believe that they are participating in reality. They are acting, but the play they are performing is more convincing than the life that gave rise to it. Thus does it happen that, unwittingly, Georges addresses the actors as if they were truly his parents and they in turn regard him as their son. Here too, in a small way, art has imposed itself upon life.

The final Anouilh work to be considered here is *Léocadia*. It is not one of the author's most effective plays, but it is worthy of attention because of its affinity to *Enrico IV*. As in the Italian drama, a man's mind becomes unbalanced by unhappiness in love—in this case, the death of his beloved—and a wealthy relative attempts to create for him a surrounding in which he can maintain the illusion that the past is not yet over. To foster the Prince's illusion that Léocadia is still alive, the Duchess re-creates on her grounds the places to which the young man had been with his love in the three days they knew each other before her death. But the Duchess then contrives a scheme to bring her nephew back to reality. She hires Amanda, a seamstress who bears a remarkable resemblance to Léocadia, to impersonate the dead beauty, hoping to shock him into the realization that Léocadia is no longer alive. The method used is exactly the same as in *Enrico IV*. The result, however, is different, for the Prince is not defeated. He comes to love Amanda and thereby succeeds in transcending the impasse of his passion for the deceased Léocadia.

If Anouilh's theater is thus found to be thoroughly imbued with Pirandello, it must not be assumed that his plays are copies of the latter's. Henri Clouard says that Anouilh "frenchifies Pirandello," [46] but he adds, as many other critics have, the names of Gérard de Nerval, Giraudoux, and especially Musset as those whose influence is seen in Anouilh. Above all stands out his own creative genius. Anouilh is no imitator. His theater is original, but, of course, no playwright writes in a vacuum. If, first, Pirandello and, second, Musset are the two strongest influences on him, it is proof of Anouilh's originality that he has been able to weld such different antecedents into a new entity bearing his own individual stamp. Anouilh's great debt to Pirandello resides in the themes that he has adapted and in the Pirandellian flavor of much of his dialogue and atmosphere. His is "a sort of Pirandellian drama of a single character in search of himself, and it reiterates the familiar theme of escape from the ugliness of life." [47]

The distinctive contribution of Anouilh is the light touch of the *pièces roses* and *pièces brillantes,* woven with strands of his peculiar irony, the more mordant humor of the *pièces grinçantes,* the characters so unreal yet alive because of their passions and their foibles. Out of these qualities is created the complex of the theater of Jean Anouilh, whose eminence among French dramatists has been achieved by a long series of thought-provoking, technically brilliant, and very actable plays.

Of the major authors discussed in this chapter, only Giraudoux and Guitry are dead. The others are still active and producing plays. Anouilh, especially, is still young and enjoying a greater reputation in the postwar era than in the thirties.

The writers considered in the preceding pages have one other element in common which, for the purpose of this study, is important in setting them apart from their colleagues of the past fourteen years. Achard, Salacrou, Giraudoux, Crommelynck, Guitry, Cocteau, and Anouilh all belong to the theatrical generation that felt the impact of Pirandello's conquest of the Parisian stage. Most of them have affirmed that they saw these initial performances (and undoubtedly all of them did) and have expressed their admiration for them. Many of the current group of playwrights were too young in the early and middle twenties to have seen, or at least fully appreciated, these plays. The difference is naturally of great import in the examination of Pirandello's role in France. It separates those who became acquainted with the author of *Sei personaggi* at the time of his greatest success from those who learned of him indirectly through revivals, through the printed text, and through the Pirandellism of their seniors.

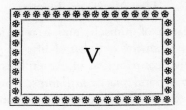

V

The French Theater: The Postwar Era

THE liberation of France in 1944 was anticlimactic to the ignoble defeat in 1940. There was some compensation in the silent heroism of the Resistance and in the frequent valor of a people subjugated by its mortal enemy. But they were not sufficient to counteract the shame that Frenchmen felt at the disintegration of their country in the face of the German lightning thrust and at the collaboration by some of their fellow citizens under the stress of a long occupation. The end of the war was cause for rejoicing but not for pride.

Moreover, hardly one year had passed before the mood of the postwar world was established. The "cold war" was preferable to the recent hot one, of course, but the distrust coupled with threats of total annihilation that it represented gave rise to cynicism and pessimism in most of a weary, abused Western Europe.

It is understandable, then, that the France which rose out of the ashes of catastrophe did not provide the proper climate for the illusions and hopes that had been entertained for some dozen blind, optimistic years following World War I, the years that it had taken to awaken to the imminence of a new disaster. This time, the process was telescoped into a period more suitably measured in months than in years, and the world quickly became aware of its precarious state.

With anarchy in world affairs, with moral values toppled by the vacuum left by the war, Existentialism left the realm of the professional philosophers and became public property. The theater achieved this transition by popularizing the complex tenets in basic terms understandable by an audience. The moment was right for widespread interest in this philosophy. If it is incorrect to label Existentialism pessimistic (as was fashionable a few years ago), it is nevertheless true that the philosophic optimism resulting from man's *engagement* and his full acceptance of his responsibilities is a bleak, unconvincing optimism, stemming from his terrible liberty of loneliness in a hostile world of absurdity.

This absurdity was no longer based on mere observation; it was the philosophic heritage of Heidegger, Jaspers, Kierkegaard, and others. As illustrated in the plays of Sartre, Beauvoir, and Camus, however, it was simplified, as befits a medium that is not basically suited to metaphysics. These dramatists stripped the absurd of its elaborate philosophic envelope, so that it emerged not unlike the absurdity of Salacrou, Anouilh, and Pirandello. In their *conception* of absurdity, the French Existentialists are indebted only to other Existentialists. But it is unlikely that they could have ever translated it to the stage successfully had it not been for the tradition initiated by Pirandello and inherited by Paris.

Nor is this the only parallel that can be drawn between the Existentialist playwrights and the Italian dramatist. Umberto

Cantoro compares the being-existence opposition to the form-life dichotomy that has been examined in Chapter II. He declares: "It will not be difficult to recognize in Pirandello's thought the outlines of Existentialism, from Kierkegaard to Heidegger, from Pascal to Marcel, from Sartre to Abbagnano. In the dualism of being and of form, there is the Existentialist dualism of being and of existing. . . ." [1] This point is well taken, for it does not claim Pirandello as an influence on Existentialist thought, but does see in him a precursor of the Existentialist theater.

Sartre, Beauvoir, and Camus are not the only prominent names of the postwar stage. In addition to the authors of the thirties whom we have examined, others, too, continued to create after the war. Two novelists, Montherlant and Mauriac, turned to the theater with great success; Malraux and Gide triumphed with their adaptations of *La Condition humaine* and *Les Caves du Vatican*, respectively. Many French versions of foreign plays were well received: Tennessee Williams, Arthur Miller, William Faulkner (in Camus' dramatization of *Requiem for a Nun*), García Lorca, and—again—Pirandello.

Meanwhile, new names were becoming well known on the Parisian stage. The plays of Adamov, Ionesco, and Neveux have won considerable attention, and Samuel Beckett's first play, *En Attendant Godot*, did more to establish his reputation than his four novels. These are but the most familiar of the rising stars; together with many others they insure vitality in the theater for years to come.

As acknowledged leader of the Existentialist school, as editor of the influential *Les Temps modernes*, as a dramatist whose plays have stirred widespread discussion, Jean-Paul Sartre is the foremost theatrical figure of the postwar era. His skill in creating a theater out of philosophical attitudes was largely responsible for the vogue of Existentialism—a remarkable achievement, for it is indeed rare when a philosophic movement enjoys real popularity, and it marks the first time that the theater was the instrument of this popularity.

Sartre's merit lies in his ability to adapt his esoteric ideas to the requirements of the stage. This transfer necessitates simplification and a choice of theatrical illustrations: Sartre the philosopher has never hesitated to do the former and Sartre the playwright possesses the artistry required for the latter. As a result, his plays can be enjoyed by the uninitiated and by those opposed to his ideas. A pioneer in a virgin field, Sartre has set high standards for those in the future who would wish to propagandize a philosophy in the theater.

Sartre has left no doubt about what he considers to be Pirandello's influence in France. Recently asked who was the most timely modern dramatist, the author of *Le Diable et le Bon Dieu* answered "It is most certainly Pirandello." [2] And, indeed, that Pirandello is very much up to date is borne out in Sartre's own theater.

For example, underlying his plays is an attack on all pretense in human behavior that tends to turn men away from the full acceptance of their responsibilities. This may be equated to Pirandello's concern with pretense as a danger when it harms others. The climaxes in Sartre's dramas occur as the main characters, breaking through the fictitious armor in which they have been clothed, face themselves and their acts in the stark glare of their liberty. In similar situations, the Sicilian's characters suffer the human anguish of self-confrontation; the Frenchman's feel the Existentialist anguish of full responsibility. In the mirror in which the former see their souls, the latter see the absurdity of life.

In *Les Mouches* (1943), the illusion of guilt is fostered on

Argos by Aegisthus and Clytemnestra, with Jupiter the instrument of their deception. The God explains that he creates this enslavement - through - make - believe by hypnotism: "I have been dancing in front of men for a hundred thousand years. A slow and somber dance. They must look at me: as long as they have their eyes fixed on me, they forget to look within themselves. If I forgot myself for a single moment, if I let them turn away their eyes. . . ." [3] It is Orestes' role to stop the dance and thereby shatter the illusion of culpability that has enthralled the citizens. By killing the royal couple, the hero takes upon his shoulders all the guilt and all the responsibility for past events. He lifts the collective mask of the populace and forces existence on them.

Inès performs the same function in *Huis clos* (1944). The only one of the play's unholy trio of characters to see clearly her own reality, she taunts the other two until all their illusions are unmasked. "Here we are stark naked," [4] she says, referring to that same nakedness that is Ersilia Drei's and that of other Pirandellian characters agonizing in self-revelation. Inès possesses the keen insight and the sharp tongue required to make Gracin and Estelle see precisely what they are, what they have done, and how they have concealed their truths behind the pretense of respectability. "Hell is Other People," [5] only because they are each other's conscience, the constant reminder of their sordid reality.

Inès, too, tears down the illusion that life is still possible in the infernal Second Empire drawing room. She makes clear that their visions of the earth are fading, that they have to stay together forever, and that the absurdity of their coexistence is complete because, being dead, they cannot even kill one another. The three have no choice but to accept the consequences of their lives, as Enrico IV had no choice but to accept his.

The illusions must be replaced by reality because they have

hurt other people. This is the same criterion for behavior that Pirandello expressed consistently. "Certainly the characters in *No Exit* 'half lucid and half overcast' strip themselves naked and wallow in their anguish much as Pirandello's six characters." [6] Garcin and the Father of *Sei personaggi* express the same objection to being judged on the basis of one isolated act. The Father feels that the Step-Daughter had caught him in a brief, unrepresentative moment of his existence and was trying to attach his entire reality to that moment. Garcin, for his part, asks "Can one judge a life on a single act?" and Inès replies tersely "Why not." [7] Likewise, in *Morts sans sépulture,* Canoris states: "It is on our whole life that each one of your acts will be judged." [8] In Garcin's case, however, that one act is not truly isolated; Inès proves it to be part of his general pattern. Cowardice is his reality and heroism merely the illusion he had created for himself. Because his wife had suffered from this illusion, Garcin is guilty and is relegated to the hell of Inès' probings.

"The anguished situation, the climate of torment in *Six Characters* is common to all of Sartre's plays and within it Sartre's heroes attempt to realize themselves like Pirandello's partially constructed characters. . . ." [9] *Morts sans sépulture* (1946) points this out also. The Resistance fighters of the play are placed by Sartre in a situation of extreme stress and torture, wherein they see clearly into their own selves. It is a terrible moment of truth for them. Some come face to face with the image of their cowardice for the first time; others discover that their heroism is tainted by dubious motives. Even those whose valor remains unchallenged find themselves drained of true human emotions, their bond to mankind severed by their singular bravery, which sets them above all others. They represent the epitome of suffering as conceived by Pirandello.

The mirror and the face behind the mask shift to the

domain of politics in the masterful denunciation of the degrad-
ing sophistry of Communist ideology—*Les Mains sales* (1948).
The reality that is revealed to Hugo does not concern his
self; it concerns the truth about the Party. Hoederer's death
is the catalyst. Upon his release from prison, Hugo learns
that the man he had killed at the Party's orders has been
"rehabilitated" posthumously. His act of murdering a man
he respected emerges futile and absurd and the Party a ruthless
tyrant with no use for idealism. Nurtured on the illusions of
Communist justice, Hugo suffers as much in his disenchantment as Pirandello's most moving characters. His *raison d'être*
has been destroyed and he goes willingly to his death.

Le Diable et le Bon Dieu (1951) is the example of the
shattering of metaphysical illusion. What Goetz attempts to
do in this epic of atheism is to rid the world of its illusion
of God and force men to behold themselves in all their liberty.
It is still basically the same theme of Existential man emerg-
ing from behind pretense to assume his responsibility and
freedom.

By 1955, *Nekrassov* proved that Sartre had lived to regret
Les Mains sales. His change of allegiance to the totalitarianism
he had condemned and his recent public repudiation of the
Soviet Union would indicate that the author frequently shares
his characters' inability to differentiate between fact and fiction. Perhaps his by now frequent reversals would not prove
so embarrassing if he did not mark each stage of his vacilla-
tion with a play that lasts longer than his latest attitude.

While *Les Mains sales* was a serious, dramatically effective
demonstration of the bankruptcy of Communist methods,
Nekrassov is a farcical attack on anti-Communists, naïve in its
conception and puerile in its argument. Again the device of
illusion is used—a newspaperman's scheme to boost circulation
by "creating" a Soviet minister who has escaped and is selling

his memoirs. It is a gigantic hoax that he tries to impose on his readers for the sake of his job, notwithstanding the international discord that can arise out of the deception.

Sartre shares two elements with Pirandello: the absurdity both men discern in life and the frequent repetition of the illusion-reality theme. The French writer has, however, penetrated to attitudes underlying the dichotomy and charged it with the implications of Existential thought. Sartre's high opinion of Pirandello, placing him at the head of modern authors, is explained by the similarities in their works—similarities which are actually far greater than a superficial glance would suggest.

In the last few years Albert Camus has replaced Sartre as the most discussed and most highly regarded French author. If his theater remains too abstract and lacks Sartre's dramatic flair, his novels, or *récits* as he prefers to call them, and his long essay, *L'Homme révolté*, have demonstrated his remarkable gifts. After a period of adhering to Existentialist thought of a more or less orthodox nature, Camus veered away from it somewhat toward a broader humanism. Always aware of the utter absurdity of man's existence in this world, he is not content to accept this absurdity—his answer is revolt. This revolt is the solidifying bond of mankind, the simple "no" that expresses the refusal to accept the unreasoning tyranny of fate. The positive values that emerge out of unblinking recognition of man's situation are Camus' specific contribution to contemporary literature.

The absurd is the bond between Pirandello and Camus. As is the case with Sartre, Camus understands the absurd in clearer and more conceptual terms than does Pirandello. Human values are implicit in Camus' theater, and perhaps because these values are never explicit, it remains too impersonal, too systematic, and too abstract. These factors certainly have been responsible for denying his theater the unqualified success of his other works.

Caligula (1945) is probably Camus' best endeavor in the dramatic medium. The Roman Emperor, who concludes that only arbitrary action can overcome the absurdity of existence, is a pathetic figure of defeat as he realizes finally that his liberty of peremptory terror was delusion because it was gained at other people's expense. Francis Jeanson compares this play to Enrico IV because both heroes are alike in their isolation despite their omnipotence in their own realms.

> One will agree that from Henry IV (1922) to Caligula (1945), the essential preoccupations and themes did not become basically different. It is very much the same denunciation of this world which is not what it ought to be; the same disdain for those who get along with it; the same feeling of solidity; the same pessimism; the same recourse to the choice of the absurd against the very absurdity of existence; the same frenzy of denying and destroying, of pulling the world out from under the feet of those who have them firmly planted on it.[10]

This statement points out very correctly the similarities between these plays. One must add, however, that the problem of responsibility, which is basic to Caligula, does not figure in Enrico IV.

One conversation between Caligula and his friend, Chéréa, is notable for its Pirandellian character:

> CALIGULA: Chéréa, do you think that two men whose souls and whose pride are equally great can, at least once in their lives, speak to each other absolutely frankly—as if they were naked, face to face, stripped of the prejudices, of the personal interests, of the lies by which they live?
> CHÉRÉA: I think that it is possible, Caïus. But I believe you are incapable of it.

CALIGULA: You are right. I only wanted to know if you thought as I do. Let us cover our faces with masks, therefore. Let us use our lies. Let us speak to each other the way people fight, covered up to the hilt. Chéréa, why don't you like me?

CHÉRÉA: Because I understand you too well and because one cannot like that face which one tries to mask in oneself.[11]

The references to masks concealing the reality of a person, to Chéréa's several faces, to the pretense in the relations between people, are very reminiscent of the Italian dramatist. Whether they stem from Camus' knowledge of Pirandello cannot be determined, but they are certainly attributable to him indirectly, for these ideas had, by 1945, become thoroughly naturalized in the French theater.

If, as we have attempted to show in the preceding pages, there is a bond between the absurdity that Pirandello portrays in personal terms and the one that the Existentialists visualize as an impersonal metaphysical reality, there is definitely a bond between the former and Samuel Beckett's *Weltanschauung*. The depiction of absurdity as the dominant aspect of life in *En Attendant Godot* is so devastating and heart-rending because it is seen, as Pirandello saw it, in a profoundly human light, tempered with compassion for the victims caught in its web.

Vladimir and Estragon symbolize mankind. Their pathetic efforts to distract each other in their never-ending wait for salvation are an attempt to create the illusion that they really exist, while actually they are merely dangling helplessly at the end of the perfidious rope of life. The great merits of the play are the ultimate *reductio ad absurdum* of the human condition and, despite the prevalent nonsensical atmosphere, its deeply moving quality on the individual level. In this respect, Beckett has contributed something new to the stage.

Fin de partie (1957) continues in the same vein, but it is even blacker in mood, less humorous, less humanistic in conception.

Pirandello had elicited compassion in his plays, but he did not aim at a generalized philosophy of absurdity; the Existentialists dramatized the absurdity of man's existence in this world without ever feeling pity for that trapped humanity; Beckett achieves the synthesis of both. His universal truth prevents him neither from sympathizing with mankind nor from participating in its fate. This reverting to the humanistic tradition is of primary importance in this postwar French theater, which tends too much to the abstract. It may explain Jean Anouilh's great enthusiasm at the opening of *En Attendant Godot:* "I think that the evening at the Babylone [Theater] is as important as the first Pirandello produced by Pitoëff in Paris in 1923." [12]

Arthur Adamov, whose reputation has been made in experimental theaters since 1950, reduces absurdity to the everyday life of ordinary people. His universe is often akin to the world of George Orwell's *1984*—a world in which the citizen is helpless against forces which victimize him for no purpose and in a haphazard way. Adamov depicts the anguish and the senseless terror of the police-state age. His pessimism is so overwhelming that he envisages life for the individual as only an illusion of reason until total absurdity annihilates it.

This horror of the modern totalitarian state is dramatized in *Tous contre tous* (1952) and *La grande et la petite manœuvre* (1950). Le Mutilé, the principal character—for one cannot speak of "heroes" in Adamov's works—of the latter play, is deprived of all his limbs, one by one, in a senseless persecution by the authorities. Still he maintains the illusion that life holds happiness for him because a woman, Erna, loves him. The reality of the chaos of existence becomes clear for him only at the end as Erna, in an act fully as gratuitous as the quadruple amputation, vilifies him and pushes him out onto the street on his caster—a pathetic stump of flesh facing certain death. He brings to mind Kafka's Joseph K., who was also destroyed by an impassive fate without ever understanding why.

Although he does not use devices that tend to bring the audience "into" the play, Adamov attempts to make the play transcend the limitations of the stage in order to confront the spectators directly. He achieves this effect by means of what one might call an ultrarealistic technique—that is, not the faithful reproduction of realism, nor the emphasis on sordidness of modern neo-realism, nor again the suggestion of a superior reality of surrealism, but a fusion of all three, in which the complete naturalness of the dialogue (to the exclusion of all theatricality), together with the sharp, brutal outline of authority, infers the ultimate absurdity.

Because the language seems spontaneous and because both the situations and the terror are products of a society that is no longer fictitious but is already developing, the audience can identify with the action without an undue effort of the imagination. As a result, the stage itself becomes more than the traditional boards, curtain, scenery, etc.; it becomes the willing accomplice of the dramatist, inasmuch as the play is projected *by means of* the stage rather than *on* the stage and is thus given life. Insofar as this is possible in a medium which, despite all efforts, is still artificial, Adamov succeeds, obtaining an additional, convincing dimension out of his stage. "The precursors whom Adamov admits besides [Antonin] Artaud . . . are all playwrights who grasped and gave material expression to the idea of the theater as an autonomous art inseparable from the physical space of the stage: Kleist, . . . Büchner, Strindberg, and Pirandello." [13]

In two plays mentioned above, Pirandello's influence is re-

stricted to the concept that the life we live is mere illusion and
to the heritage of absurdity. It is more widespread in other
works. *L'Invasion* (1950) stresses the relative nature of truth
in a world wherein absolute truth is impossible to attain. The
title refers to an unfinished manuscript which intrudes into
the life of the family and friends of its deceased author. The
laborious struggle of these people to decipher the handwriting
and clarify the work ends in a dismal stalemate, for, in addition to disagreeing among themselves, they individually find
different interpretations for each word until no one is certain
of the real meaning. The chief would-be editor finally tears
up the manuscript and dies, an apparent suicide. The symbol
of the enigmatic opus, whose meaning is impervious to com-
prehension, is akin to Signora Frola's veil, emphasizing the
impossibility of determining the truth.

La Parodie (1952) suggests again that life is lived in an
illusion, with reality hidden and far removed. The motions
of the characters in the play are, like our own motions, only
a parody of existence itself. Lastly, *Le Professeur Taranne*
(1953), concerns a Pirandellian type of self-confrontation.
The university scholar of the title is incapable of living up to
his reputation, and as he grows aware of the gap between
his true self and the person he is thought to be, he resorts to
plagiarizing the ideas of his colleague Ménard. But Taranne
cannot endure his own deception any more than he could
endure mediocrity. Subconsciously craving to be exposed, he
carries to an extreme the act of stripping himself of all deceit;
he is caught walking the streets stark naked. He thus shows
his true self without the illusions imposed by the plagiary.
Ironically, people mistake Taranne for Ménard when he tries
to identify himself. The illusion has even conquered others.

It is evident that Pirandello's ideas infiltrate these five plays
in varying degrees. While Adamov added his personal quali-

ties, he remained very true to the Italian's concepts. His theater is compelling and almost frighteningly modern in its
emphasis on the suppression of the individual and on the
impossibility of communication between people. The absurdity
of contemporary life, seen in abstract terms in Beckett's plays,
is very concretely pictured in the theater of Arthur Adamov.

Eugène Ionesco represents, together with Adamov and
Beckett, the successful new voice in the French theater.* His
plays place him with the writers of the absurd, but the world
of Ionesco lacks the brutality of Adamov or the total despair of
Beckett. He does share with the latter one quality, rare indeed
among innovators today—humor. Much of his work is filled
with jokes, puns, amusing nonsense, and apparently meaning-
less sentences that are often uproarious.

His first play, *La Cantatrice chauve* (1950), seems to have
the same basic goal as Adamov's *La Parodie*. Like his elder
colleague, Ionesco calls attention to the mechanical ritual of
living, which creates the illusion of life but which, in fact, is
only a parody of it. His subject is that often satirized English
society of proverbial reserve, lack of humor, vapid social banter,
and sentimentality. Despite the absurdity of the dialogue and
the situations, *La Cantatrice chauve* is really a hilarious play,
proving that social criticism can be amusing.

In *Les Chaises* (1952) and *Amédée ou Comment s'en
débarasser* (1952), Ionesco deals with the married couple. Of
these two, the first play moves on a real and on an illusory
level. Amédée and his wife Madeleine find a dead man in
their apartment. While this corpse, symbolic of the love that
they have killed in each other, grows constantly, taking up

---

* It is interesting to note that all three men stem from countries other
than France. Ionesco was born in Rumania, Beckett in Ireland, Adamov
in Russia.

more and more room in their apartment, until it becomes gigantic, the couple continues to behave in an entirely normal way as if the situation were completely natural. In other words, the illusion of the enlarging body becomes a part of their everyday reality.

Les Chaises projects the interior existence of a very old couple onto a semicircular stage, which soon fills with chairs. These chairs are occupied by imaginary guests, including the Emperor, entertained by the old man and woman. Whereas the illusion in *Amédée* is materialized as a corpse, in *Les Chaises* it is left an illusion: the increasing number of imaginary people are reflected only by the ever larger number of chairs that clutter the stage. Besides this Pirandellian illusion theme, Ionesco suggests also the multiplicity of the old woman's personality. Suddenly, she becomes grotesque and vulgar, and the stage direction demands "a style of acting completely different from the one she has used up to now and from the one she is to use afterwards, and which is meant to reveal a hidden personality in the old woman." [14] This is her erotic self coming to the fore.

Ionesco, like Beckett and Adamov, attempts to use the theater for new, essentially dramatic expression. These three authors and other *avant-garde* playwrights like Neveux, Genet, and Vauthier approach the play primarily as a function of the theater. Therefore, they investigate every avenue of theatricality and invention that might extend the limits of the stage. In Pirandello they found a logical precursor who had tried the same thing. Ionesco explains that "Luigi Pirandello's theater does, in fact, meet the ideal exigencies of the structure, of the dynamic architecture of the drama. He is the manifestation of the inalterable archetype of the idea of the theater which we have in us. . . ." [15]

Brief mention should be made of *L'Autre Alexandre* (1957), a play essentially in the experimental tradition, by Marguerite Libéraki, who has not yet reached prominence as a playwright. She, too, delves into personality structure and does so by the novel process of creating a set of illegitimate brothers and sisters to match, down to the very names, a set of legitimate half-siblings. The effect is like a mirror placed in front of this family: the reflections are at once so similar and so different that they appear to be reality and the reflections of a single set of characters.

Although his theater is best classified as *avant-garde,* Georges Neveux is neither a young nor a recently discovered author. His *Juliette ou la Clé des songes* was written in 1927 and won him considerable renown at the time of its production in 1930. *Ma Chance et me chanson,* his next play, did not follow until 1940, and since then he has written regularly for the stage.

The experimental element of Neveux's works is the technique: the dramatization of a heavily symbolic dream; the encounter with the dead, the living, and the unborn; the face-to-face meeting of a man and his self; the experiencing of an action before it takes place. The content of his theater is, however, surprisingly traditional. His subjects are fate and the human experiences of life and death. Neveux is not a philosophical playwright, and one need not seek a system of thought or a portrayal of the absurd in his dramas. Germaine Brée points out that the "bitter existential revolt against man's 'absurd' condition is completely alien to him. In *Plainte contre inconnu* [1946] he reverses the basic existentialist theme, pointing to the 'absurd' human refusal to accept life, all of life, as it is given." [16] This emphasis on life's positive values is in welcome opposition to the gloom of most of Neveux's fellow *avant-gardistes*.

We have noted previously (p. 49) that Neveux assigned to *Sei personaggi* an enormous influence in the history of the modern French theater. Recently, on the occasion of the twentieth anniversary of Pirandello's death, a French periodical asked several French playwrights if they had been influenced by Pirandello. Georges Neveux's answer explains not only what he himself, but also what an entire generation of French dramatists, found in Pirandello:

> Pirandello is, first of all, the greatest prestidigitator of the Twentieth Century, the Houdini of interior life. In his most important play, *Six Characters*, he took the very center of the real world and turned it inside out right in front of us, as the fisherman turns inside out the skin of an octopus to lay bare its viscera.
>
> But what Pirandello laid bare before us is not only the work of the actors, nor that of the author, not only the other side of the scenery, but something much more universal: *the other side of ourselves.*
>
> It is our inner life which is suddenly found projected on the stage and decomposed there as if by a prism.
>
> What are these fantoms, condemned to relive endlessly the same scene (all of a sudden one thinks of *Huis clos*) if not the most obscure part of ourselves? These six characters are not only the unfinished creatures of an author at a creative impasse, but also, and more important still, those impulses which each of us keeps within him and does not manage to live out.[17]

This sudden confrontation with one's inner self and these hidden desires are the Pirandellian elements in Neveux's theater. His Pirandellism is always on the human level; he is not concerned with the artist's dilemma.

In *Le Voyage de Thésée* (1943), the Minotaur that Theseus finds in the labyrinth of Cnossus looks like Theseus him-

self; it is, in fact, an aspect—the happy side—of the young
Athenian's personality which suddenly confronts him. The
secret of the Minotaur's deadly power over the many youths
sent yearly to slay it was its ability to appear as the hidden self
of each of its victims, which paralyzed them in the agony of
this encounter. Theseus alone has the strength to look at himself honestly, to reject, by tearing the thread linking him to
his bride, that Theseus who longs for happiness, and to accept his fate by recognizing it in the labyrinth of this existence.
The Pirandellian mirror in *Le Voyage de Thésée* is the Minotaur.

Self-confrontation is achieved in a more conventional
manner in *Plainte contre inconnu* (1946). The six plaintiffs
against God or the Unknown—who appear in the prosecutor's
office as gratuitously as do Pirandello's six characters on the
stage, and who, like them, demand to register their protest
against the injustices done to them—are dissuaded from their
planned suicide by being afforded a long look at themselves.
This is made possible indirectly by the prosecutor. Having
attempted and failed to change the determination of the sextet
bent on self-destruction with the customary reasons in favor
of life, the public servant unwittingly offers them hope. He
points out what a perfectly happy man he is, shielded from
any conceivable annoyance or misfortune. In so doing, he
lays bare the empty existence of a man whose impervious
armor shelters nothing within him. Upon seeing what a
"happy" man looks like, the six reconsider their decision.
Each of them searches deeply within himself and realizes that
life is worth being lived: they all choose to resume their lives.
The image of his own hollowness is not lost on the poor prosecutor either, and it is he who finally shoots himself.

Additional Pirandellian elements can be observed in
Neveux's other plays. Although the employee of the dream

bureau in *Juliette ou la Clé des songes* makes it clear that dreams and reality must remain in mutually exclusive worlds for a sane man, Neveux nevertheless punctuates the attraction existing between them. For Michel, the illusory realm of Juliette has far greater appeal than the life in which Juliette escaped him. He is reluctant to abandon his travels, through the symbolist maze for the less enchanting, if truer, light of the everyday world.

In *Ma Chance et ma chanson*, the dead materialize on the scene when they are needed with the same sort of improvised magic that brings forth Madama Pace in *Sei personaggi*. Lastly, one element of *Zamore* (1953) also evokes the Italian play. With the help of *la fièvre de tout à l'heure* ("the in-a-little-while-fever"), a condition that enables one to see the near future, the Police Commissioner tells Zamore that he will be killed by Charles Auguste, his wife's lover. From that point on, try as they will to escape their fate, the curious *ménage à trois* plunges relentlessly forward in their destined roles with as little real hope of avoiding the culminating shot as there is for the six characters. The three are, in fact, like characters falling in spite of themselves into the trap an author has set for them.

Neveux's use of Pirandellian techniques and motifs is a good example of how modern playwrights—even of the *avant-garde*—benefited from Pirandello. He is certainly not an imitator, and none of his plays is overwhelmingly in the Italian's tradition; but Neveux's theater as a whole incorporates much of what is best in Pirandello.

Jean Genet's *Les Bonnes* (1946) dramatizes a double transfer of personality. The sisters Claire and Solange, Madame's maids, engage in frequent excursions into other personalities, with one "playing" their employer, the other taking her sister's role. On the day of the action, it is Claire who, as Madame, heaps abuse on Solange, whom she calls Claire. What had started as a game for the sisters has become starkly real. With the "imitation Madame" wearing the clothes and assuming the manner of speaking of the actual Madame, the two lash one another with their tongues and verbalize their resentment against their mistress. Their occasional lapses, when they call each other by their true rather than their assumed names, stress only more strongly how fully immersed they are in their adopted identities. Having prepared a poisoned tea for the real Madame without succeeding in getting her to drink it, Claire, completely consumed by her impersonation, drinks the fatal brew.

By accepting Madame's death, Claire fuses into Madame's personality. This alter ego—only an illusion at first—is complete reality at the end. Genet's view of disintegrating personality is directly in the Pirandellian line, with the emphasis on the imagined aspect of multiplicity rather than on the innate one.

The last of the experimental authors to be considered in relation to Pirandello is Jean Vauthier. Written in 1955 and produced by Jean-Louis Barrault the following year, *Le Personnage combattant (fortissimo)* is an interesting examination of the creative process. Vauthier presents us with an author—Le Personnage—who returns to a provincial hotel room where, fifteen years earlier, he had begun a novel about the poetic awakening of a young man, Georges Pellermann. Le Personnage attempts to rewrite and complete his work, but in the process he becomes painfully aware of the change that has taken place in him in the interim. He now sees, as did * * * of *Quando si è qualcuno*, that his renown is not deserved. In the mirror of his early manuscript, the author observes the degeneration that has taken place within him. He spends a tortured night trying to write, trying to recapture his youth, trying to accept himself as he is now. After his ranting and screaming, the agony ends at daybreak with a calm that promises renewed vigor for the author.

Le Personnage combattant attempts to dramatize the actual process of writing—probably the ultimate outgrowth of Pirandello's trilogy. But Vauthier fails to make it theatrical enough. He writes of his debt to the Italian: "It is Pirandello's extraordinary dramatic intensity that reached me and 'landed on me.' " [18] But it is precisely Pirandello's extraordinary dramatic intensity that is needed and not fully felt here. Except for a few lines spoken by the bellboy, the play is a long monologue interrupted only by the noises of the railroad and the neighbors. The spectator tires of this ever-present Personnage, and little by little loses sympathy for him. The subject matter is nondramatic and the treatment equally nondramatic. Jean Renoir, in *Orvet* (see p. 143) treats essentially the same subject, but succeeds, because he brings the writing out of the author's mind and makes it come alive on the stage.

It would seem that Vauthier found his character in much the same way that Pirandello had been accosted by his six characters: "I found my character in between two texts. This character animated a theme which I had been carrying in me for a long time, he constructed the play, he gave rise to each event." [19] But he never allows his Personnage to live, because his dramatic skill was not suited to the task. Perhaps *Le Personnage combattant* suffers simply from excess experimentation.

La Fugue de Caroline (1945), by Alfred Adam, deserves some attention only because of its Pirandellian viewpoint. The play itself is weak and of no major importance. It concerns Alexis and Agathe, a married couple who bicker incessantly about each other's ancestors, whose portraits hang in their house. In what is apparently Alexis' dream, the portraits come to life and take up the argument about their respective families. The biggest point of contention: Why did ancestor Caroline run away on her wedding day? With the help of another ancestor, who serves as *metteur-en-scène*, they re-create the past, which reveals that Caroline, having been led to believe that her lover is dead, has been tricked into marriage. When her lover returns on Caroline's wedding day, she tries to drown herself, but he rescues her and takes her away. The mystery solved, the ancestors return to their frames and Alexis and Agathe are left with their fury somewhat abated.

Various Pirandellian themes crisscross through *La Fugue de Caroline*: There is a play (Caroline's story) within a dream (the portraits) within the play (Alexis and Agathe). There is an intermingling of illusion and reality in the contrast between the portraits and the portraits-in-search-of-their-past and also in Alexis' mystical relation to the portraits. There is, lastly, an emphasis on the multiplicity of the self: two of the ancestors appear in double form, and Agathe tells her husband, "You do not understand, then, that each day a new Agathe emanates from the preceding one, until it reaches the last Alexis. . . ." [20]

Although he states that he does not like the play, Francis Ambrière, in his reviews of plays from 1945 to 1948, somehow manages to praise it by saying that "the idea is excellent, and it is a pleasant attempt, although not very new, after Pirandello, to materialize the splittings of the personality." [21] It is true that there is nothing original in *La Fugue de Caroline*, but the idea can hardly be called excellent; it is too artificial, too confused, and too pointless. At best, one might agree with the word agreeable. All in all, this play is an example of those imitations of Pirandello that add nothing new and do not use the old material with any particular distinction.

The art medium most closely associated with Jean Renoir is the cinema. He is, in fact, one of the directors who have made it possible to use the word "art" in this connection. Renoir is mentioned here because of his play, *Orvet,* produced in Paris in 1955, which is completely Pirandellian in ideas, style, and technique.

Several years previously, he had already indicated his predilection for the Italian's theater in the film *Le Carrosse d'or,* directed and partially written by Renoir, based on Mérimée's *Le Carrosse du Saint-Sacrement.* This story of a *commedia dell'arte* company touring eighteenth-century South America is told on even more levels than Pirandello's trilogy. It is a play-within-a-play-within-a-film. The opening scene portrays a theater whose curtain lifts and on whose stage takes place the balance of the action. This action is on twin levels: the trials and tribulations of Columbina, the leading actress, with a soldier, a bullfighter, and the viceroy; and the plays performed by the actors. These two distinct spheres become intermingled as the "life" situations are repeated in the improvisations of the players, who, in turn, take a role in solving the amorous difficulties of those situations. At the end, the theater curtain falls and the actress who played Columbina-the-actress is told by her leading man not to become so involved in this story, because, after all, the play is only illusion. But, in a last proof of the proximity between reality and illusion, the actress confesses that she regrets the three men who had courted "her."

Le Carrosse d'or is constructed in three concentric circles—the *commedia dell'arte* performances inside the play inside the film. When concentric circles begin to spin, they create the optical illusion of blending into one another. This same illusion is created by Renoir as the three circles fuse and overlap. The interplay between performance and reality is effected in the direct Pirandellian tradition.

Renoir explains how he became aware of Pirandello's importance: "I attended one of the first performances of *Six Characters* by the Pitoëffs. I was delighted, but Pirandello's importance became clear to me later, on reading him." [22] He further discusses his own relation to the Italian: "Pirandello influenced most of the modern authors. . . . He opened a new window on the infinite horizons of the collective imagination, and, like so many others, I certainly breathed some of that air." [23] It is not surprising then that Renoir's venture into the legitimate theater was very decidedly Pirandellian.

Orvet is at once a charming modernized version of Hans Christian Andersen's tale, *The Little Mermaid,* and a study of the obstacles that encumber the creative artist. As in *Sei personnagi* and *Ciascuno a suo modo*—which *Orvet* resembles in many ways—the format is, again, a play-within-a-play, with two interweaving planes of reality.

Georges, a playwright, retires to his country house to write his dramatization of the Andersen fable. He meets a simple sixteen-year-old girl of the woods, Orvet, whom he had known when they were both much younger. Despite her outward crudity, he spies a gem beneath the rustic exterior, but he lacks the audacity to make advances to her. He then approaches his play and creates first Olivier, the prince of his new version. Renoir's portrayal of the creative process is rare artistry. Olivier appears as the various preliminary sketches Georges makes of his character. He rejects Olivier the rich man and Olivier the painter, and then he realizes that "I am wrong to try to give a profession to this character before knowing what

he is like." [24] Thereupon Olivier appears, a *personnage* created
by an author but whose character and fate depend on the
"life" he himself will live. "You are the master!" Olivier tells
Georges, who replies, "No. Above all, not the master. I am a
more experienced friend . . . an adviser. . . ." [25]

Before creating the girl, Georges reads Andersen out loud
and evokes the mermaid. Orvet promptly appears out of his
mind to present herself as his mermaid. Her acts and words
duplicate those she had really used in the opening scene.
Georges' last act as author is to introduce Orvet to Olivier—
whom he has made his nephew. Although they are not attracted to each other at first, Georges refuses to interfere any
longer. The characters are now on their own and he tells them
that "the rest only depends on you. I am leaving." [26]

From that point on, love comes to Orvet and Olivier. He
will take her to Paris with him, thus removing her from
her element of the forest, as the Prince in the fairy-tale had
lured her out of the water. The inevitable heartbreak that
Georges had foreseen occurs, as Olivier tires of her and rejects
her. Only Georges finds that he has far more than an author's
interest in his story. He has, in fact, fallen in love with his
Orvet, but he is powerless. His character has escaped him and
he cannot force her to love him: "Once again I am the victim
of that dilemma which all authors must face. Either we remain
the master of the characters—in that case they never exceed
the mentality of marionettes. Or we give them life, that is to
say the right to discuss, and they drag us beyond the limits
of imagination. . . ." [27]

This is the perennial dilemma facing the writer, as stated
by Pirandello in the Preface to *Sei personaggi*. By making his
characters real, the author loses dominion over them; yet it
is his only way of creating. As Georges sees Orvet, heartbroken,

belonging now neither to the woods nor to the city, he understands the creative failure that is the lot of all playwrights:

> Dear God, forgive me for having been proud . . . for hav-
> ing tried to usurp your functions. . . . Forgive me for having
> attempted to do something which is only in your realm:
> to create . . . to create life . . . I admit my impotence.
> . . . I was not able to endow Orvet with the carefree indiffer-
> ence which would slowly cure her of her lost love.[28]

The author sees only one way out: because all his characters
live in his imagination he will make them vanish. "I am going
to give you all a wonderful gift," he tells them, "the most beautiful gift which an apprentice-creator can give to his creatures:
I am going to choose that moment when you believe in the
illusion of happiness, to send you back into nothingness." [29]
Realizing that they are only figments of his mind, the characters protest that Georges should have made them differently.
But, at last, they disappear willingly. Before the curtain falls,
Orvet, the real Orvet, enters, and this time Georges does not
neglect to do what he had not done in his play and what
Olivier had done: he tells her she is beautiful, and he asks to
kiss her hand.

It need hardly be stressed that Renoir's consideration of the
artistic process and of life altered by illusion is entirely Pirandellian. Georges' play springs to life like the strange tale in
Sei personaggi; the play triumphs over reality, as it did in
Ciascuno a suo modo, since the author falls in love with his
creation, and this love is continued beyond the limits of the
play. The action of *Orvet* is more or less equivalent to what
Pirandello tells us in the Preface about the six characters.
Renoir also brings characters to life and then rejects them
by effacing them from his mind. But because they now have
their own existence, one may say, using the Sicilian's phrase,

that they survive the end of the drama as characters in search of an author, waiting to have their story resolved. Renoir has actually added one more dimension to the Pirandellian theater-within-the-theater as a reflection of the problem of creation.

Thus Pirandello penetrates most of the important new modes of dramatic expression in the postwar era: the Existentialist theater, the *avant-garde* theater, and that unclassifiable theater of imagination exemplified by Jean Renoir. It seems particularly significant that Pirandello's influence is quite strong on the experimental playwrights. In a dynamic theater, such as the French, there is constant evolution, and it seems probable that these playwrights are now pointing the way to the drama of the rising generation. In several more years, it will, no doubt, be possible to distinguish between the immediate postwar theater and, perhaps, a theater of the late fifties. With Ionesco, Beckett, Adamov, Vauthier, and others marking the start of this transformation, Pirandellian concepts appear destined to play a major role in the future. They certainly have been important to dramatists of the first fifteen years following World War II, and they show undiminished vigor and appeal. Until, and unless, the French theater revolts completely and rejects all that has been done in the past thirty-seven years, Pirandello will remain one of its leading figures.

Pirandello has been applauded enthusiastically in France since the initial performances of *La Volupté de l'honneur* and *Six Personnages en quête d'auteur,* and his techniques and propositions have been mirrored with equal enthusiasm by many French playwrights. French plays depicting the relativity of truth, the multiplicity of personality, the art-life opposition, and the overwhelming absurdity of life have become familiar on the Parisian stage during the past three and one half decades. The striking modernity of his approach appealed to many French dramatists, and the lessons Pirandello taught them were taken seriously. His influence reached a considerable segment of dramatic authors both great and secondary. It was with only slight exaggeration that Georges Neveux said:

> Without Pirandello and without the Pitoëffs (because one can no longer separate them, the genius of the Pitoëffs having given its form to Pirandello's) we would have had neither Salacrou, nor Anouilh, nor today Ionesco, nor . . . [sic] but I shall stop, this enumeration would be endless. The entire theatre of an era came out of the womb of that play, *Six Characters.*[30]

A great part of the French theater of our era was, in fact, influenced in one way or another by Pirandello, or showed certain similarities to his. Some playwrights, like Anouilh, are Pirandellian in a major group of their plays; others, like Cocteau, only in one or two plays. While many were directly influenced, others found that their ideas were in accord with his, and still others—especially some of today's younger dramatists—have felt the impact indirectly through their seniors, who had already made Pirandellism a part of the French theater. Pirandello is "French" now not only because his plays have been produced regularly in Paris for the past thirty-seven years, but also because his ideas and methods were made essential elements of French dramatic expression during this period. The Sicilian is still a potent force in the contemporary scene.

It is rare for a dramatist to wield a truly extensive international influence. Besides Pirandello, only Shakespeare and Ibsen have left such a legacy, and it is unlikely that either has affected the theater of a single country of any one era more than the author of *Sei personaggi*. Of all the various forces that combined to mold the theatrical imagination of the French writers of our age, none was more widespread, none more penetrating, and none more productive than his.

The essence of Pirandello's theater is the marrow of contemporary ideas, of modern anxieties and pessimism. This is what the French writers admired in him. Elements of Pirandellism can be detected in the works of other European playwrights: László Krakatos, Kurt Goetz, Miguel de Unamuno—in whose case similarities are seen rather than influence. In this country, Pirandellian concepts might be found illustrated in the plays of Thornton Wilder, Elmer Rice, and Arthur Miller. But these are all isolated cases and indicate no concentrated influence by Pirandello on a country's theater. Even in Italy, where one might expect to find an important school of dramatists influenced by the master, only a relatively few well-known authors reflect Pirandello's contribution. One might mention Gherardo Gherardi, Ugo Betti, Eduardo de Filippo, Diego Fabbri, and Cesare Viola, but they are in no way disciples.

It was France which was most receptive to Pirandello and which adopted him as its own. The Italian, who had been most responsible for liberating his country's drama from simple imitations of French models, turned the tables by giving France bold new ideas and daring techniques. Pirandello's great role in France is an outstanding example of international theater, a challenging study in comparative literature.

CHAPTER I

1. For the biographical information, I am indebted to Domenico Vittorini's *Drama of Luigi Pirandello* (Philadelphia: Univ. of Penn. Press, 1935), Federico Vittore Nardelli's *L'Uomo segreto* (Milan: Mondadori, 1944), and Eric Bentley's Appendix II to his edition of five Pirandello plays, *Naked Masks* (New York: Dutton, 1952).

2. Eric Bentley's Appendix II to his edition of Luigi Pirandello, *Naked Masks*, p. 379.

3. *Ibid.*

4. See Camille Mallarmé, "Comment Luigi Pirandello fut révélé au public parisien le 20 décembre, 1922," *Revue de l'histoire du théâtre*, I (1955), 7–37.

5. Letter to the author, dated March 2, 1956. For contemporary periodical criticism of the Italian's plays, see J. N. Alley, "French Periodical Criticism of Pirandello's Plays," *Italica*, XXV, No. 2 (June, 1948), 138–149. All translations into English of this and subsequent non-English quotations are my own. When page numbers are given, they refer to the original language editions.

6. *Ibid.*

7. *Le Théâtre des années folles* (Geneva: Éditions du milieu du monde, 1943), pp. 34–35.

8. (Paris: Gallimard, 1935), p. 317.

9. *Retours à pied* (Paris: G. Crès, 1925), pp. 178–179.

10. Letter to the author, dated Feb. 8, 1957.

11. Alfred Mortier, *Quinze Ans de théâtre* (Paris: Albert Messein, 1933), p. 279.

12. "Le Pirandellisme," *Revue politique et littéraire*, LXIV, No. 12 (June 19, 1926), 383.

13. *Le Théâtre français contemporain* (Brussels: La Boétie, 1947), p. 272.

CHAPTER II

1. Luigi Pirandello, *Liolà; Così è (se vi pare)* (Verona: Mondadori, 1953), p. 59. In the editions of Pirandello's plays used in this book, no city of publication is given. Verona is indicated as place of printing.

2. *Ibid.*, p. 99.

3. Luigi Pirandello, *Sei personaggi in cerca d'autore; Enrico IV* (Verona: Mondadori, 1954), pp. 93–94.

4. *Ibid.*, pp. 46–47.

5. *Ibid.*, p. 46.

6. Luigi Pirandello, *Sei personaggi in cerca d'autore; Enrico IV* (Verona: Mondadori, 1954), p. 100.

7. *Ibid.*, pp. 131–132.

8. Walter Starkie, *Luigi Pirandello* (London: J. M. Dent, 1926), p. 185.

9. *Sei personaggi in cerca d'autore; Enrico IV*, p. 174.

10. Luigi Pirandello, *Vestire gli ignudi; L'Altro figlio; L'Uomo dal fiore in bocca* (Verona: Mondadori, 1951), pp. 97–98.

11. Preface to *Sei personaggi*, p. 16.

12. Lander MacClintock, *The Age of Pirandello* (Bloomington: Indiana University Press, 1951), p. 205.

13. *Op. cit.* Ch. VII is titled "Pirandello, the Perfect Pessimist."

CHAPTER III

1. Quoted in *Théâtre de France*, No. 3 (1953), 125.

2. Letter to the author by Denys Amiel, dated March 13, 1956.

3. Paul Werrie, *Le Théâtre de la fuite* (Bruxelles-Paris: Les Écrits, 1943), p. 227.

4. Silvio d'Amico, "Fortuna di Pirandello, 1936–1952," *Rivista di studi teatrali*, I, No. 3–4 (July–Dec., 1952), 261.

5. *Les Pitoëff* (Paris: Odette Lieutier, 1943), pp. 120–121.

6. Werrie, *op. cit.*, p. 188.

7. Translator's Note by Ernest Boyd in English edition of *Maya* (New York: The Actor-Managers, Inc., 1928), pp. 11–12.

8. According to Rhodes, "the prostitute Bella is transformed . . . into a Bella-Maya, into a Pirandellian heroine in whom everyone sees what he wishes her to be . . ." (S. A. Rhodes in Ch. V, "France and Belgium," in *A History of Modern Drama*, ed. Barrett Clark and George Freedley [New York: Appleton Century, 1947], p. 301).

9. Jean-Victor Pellerin, *Têtes de rechange; Intimité* (Paris: Coutan-Lambert, 1940), p. 90.

10. *Ibid.*, p. 203.

11. *Loc. cit.*

12. (Paris: Plon, 1925), p. x.

13. *Ibid.*, p. ix.

14. Letter to the author, dated March 12, 1956.

15. *Ibid.*

16. *Ibid.*

17. Maxime Chastaing, "L'Uomo come protagonista nel teatro francese contemporaneo," *Rivista di studi teatrali*, I, No. 1 (Jan.–March, 1952), 55.

18. *Op. cit.*, pp. 262–263.

19. *Op. cit.*, p. 198.

20. Henri-René Lenormand, *Mixture*, in *Théâtre complet*, VII (Paris: G. Crès, 1931), 152.

21. *Ibid.*, p. 179.

22. *Ibid.*, pp. 107–108.

23. *Ibid.*, p. 180.

24. I (Paris: Albin Michel, 1949), 327.

25. Henri-René Lenormand, *Crépuscule du Théâtre*, in *Théâtre complet*, VIII (Paris: Albin Michel, 1935), 119.

26. *Ibid.*, p. 57.

27. *Ibid.*, p. 80.

28. "Les Tendances actuelles du théâtre," *Encyclopédie française*, XVII (Dec., 1935), Ch. ii, "Les Arts du temps," iv, 1–12.

29. Letter to the author, dated March 29, 1956.

30. *The French Drama of the Unspoken* (Edinburgh: University Press, 1953), p. 199.

31. Alfred Savoir, *La Couturière de Lunéville* (Paris: Librairie théâtrale, 1923), p. 127.
32. Michel de Ghelderode, *Trois Auteurs, un drame*, in *Théâtre*, II (Paris: Gallimard, 1952), 134.
33. *Ibid.*, p. 143.
34. *Ibid.*, p. 144.
35. *Ibid.*, p. 146.
36. *Ibid.*, p. 148.

CHAPTER IV

1. *Le Théâtre des années folles*, p. 106.
2. René Lalou, *Le Théâtre en France depuis 1900* (Paris: Presses universitaires de France, 1951), p. 58; Henri Clouard, *Histoire de la littérature française*, II (Paris: Albin Michel, 1949), 436–437.
3. Rhodes, "France and Belgium," p. 17.
4. Marcel Achard, *Domino*, in *La Petite Illustration*, No. 582 (June 25, 1932), 22.
5. *Ibid.*
6. *Ibid.*, p. 26.
7. See Ch. I, note 5.
8. In "Aux écoutes," quoted on cover of *La Petite Illustration*, No. 872 (May 21, 1938).
9. Marcel Achard, *Le Corsaire*, in *La Petite Illustration*, No. 872 (May 21, 1938), 22.
10. *Ibid.*, p. 23.
11. Quoted on page 36 of *La Petite Illustration*, No. 872.
12. Armand Salacrou, *Le Pont de l'Europe*, in *Théâtre*, I (Paris: Gallimard, 1943), 174.
13. *Ibid.*, p. 149.
14. *Ibid.*, p. 116.
15. *Ibid.*, p. 117.
16. Armand Salacrou, *L'Inconnue d'Arras*, in *Théâtre*, III (Paris: Gallimard, 1942), 195.
17. *Ibid.*, p. 214.
18. Lalou, *op. cit.*, p. 74.
19. Armand Salacrou, *Poof; L'Archipel Lenoir* (Paris: Gallimard, 1950), p. 106.
20. *Ibid.*, p. 107.

21. *Op. cit.*, p. 264.

22. Jean Giraudoux, *La Folle de Chaillot* (Paris: Bernard Grasset, 1946), p. 17.

23. *Ibid.*, pp. 108–109.

24. Jean Giraudoux, *L'Impromptu de Paris* (Paris: Bernard Grasset, 1937), p. 20.

25. *Op. cit.*, pp. 53–54.

26. Letter to the author dated March 12, 1956.

27. Bentley, *Naked Masks*, p. 380.

28. Werrie, *loc. cit.*

29. Review by Colette in *Le Journal*, quoted, on cover of *La Petite Illustration, Quand jouons-nous la comédie!*, No. 763 (March 17, 1936).

30. *The Idea of a Theater* (Garden City: Doubleday, 1954), p. 209.

31. Jean Cocteau, *Les Chevaliers de la Table Ronde*, in *Théâtre*, I (Paris: Gallimard, 1948), 214.

32. Letter to the author, dated March 10, 1956.

33. Jean Anouilh, *Le Voyageur sans bagage*, in *Pièces noires* (Paris: Calmann-Lévy, 1942), p. 271.

34. *Ibid.*, p. 269.

35. *Ibid.*, p. 326.

36. Jean Anouilh, *Colombe*, in *Pièces brillantes* (Paris: La Table ronde, 1951), p. 316.

37. Jean Anouilh, *Ardèle ou la Marguerite*, in *Pièces grinçantes* (Paris: La Table ronde, 1956), p. 50.

38. Jean Anouilh, *La Répétition ou l'Amour puni*, in *Pièces brillantes*, p. 390.

39. *Ibid.*, p. 398.

40. *Ibid.*, p. 429.

41. *Ibid.*, p. 358.

42. Jean Anouilh, *Y'avait un prisonnier*, in *La Petite Illustration*, No. 274 (May 18, 1935), 9.

43. *Ibid.*, p. 18.

44. Jean Anouilh, *Le Rendez-vous de Senlis*, in *Pièces roses* (Paris: Calmann-Lévy, 1942), p. 140.

45. *Ibid.*, p. 203.

46. *Op. cit.*, p. 463.

47. Rhodes, "France and Belgium," pp. 296–297.

CHAPTER V

1. *Luigi Pirandello e il problema della personalità* (Bologna: Nicola Ugo Gallo, 1954), p. 191.

2. "À Paris et Ailleurs," *Les Nouvelles Littéraires*, No. 1286 (April 24, 1952), 7.

3. Jean-Paul Sartre, *Les Mouches*, in *Théâtre* (Paris: Gallimard, 1947), p. 78.

4. Sartre, *Huis clos*, in *Théâtre*, p. 147.

5. *Ibid.*, p. 167.

6. Richard B. Vowles, "Existentialism and Dramatic Form," *Educational Theatre Journal*, Oct., 1953, p. 217.

7. Sartre, *Huis clos*, in *Théâtre*, p. 165.

8. Sartre, *Morts sans sépulture*, in *Théâtre*, p. 246.

9. Vowles, *loc. cit.*

10. "Pirandello et Camus à travers Henri IV et Caligula," *Les Temps modernes*, No. 61 (Nov., 1950), 952.

11. Albert Camus, *Le Malentendu; Caligula* (Paris: Gallimard, 1947), p. 177.

12. "Godot ou le sketch des Pensées de Pascal traité par les Fratellini," *Arts*, No. 400 (Feb. 27–March 5, 1953), 1.

13. Carlos Lynes, Jr., "Adamov or 'le sens littéral' in the Theatre," *Yale French Studies*, XIV (Winter, 1954–1955), 56.

14. Eugène Ionesco, *Les Chaises*, in *Théâtre*, I (Paris: Gallimard, 1954), 146.

15. Eugène Ionesco, quoted in "Pirandello vous a-t-il influencé?" *Arts*, No. 602 (Jan. 16–22, 1957), 2.

16. "Georges Neveux: A Theatre of Adventure," *Yale French Studies*, XIV (Winter, 1954–1955), 67.

17. Statement by Georges Neveux in "Pirandello vous a-t-il influencé?" *Arts*, No. 602, *loc. cit.*

18. Quotation from Jean Vauthier, *ibid.*

19. "Notes de l'Auteur," in Jean Vauthier, *Le Personnage combattant (fortissimo)* (Paris: Gallimard, 1955), pp. 15–16.

20. Alfred Adam, *La Fugue de Caroline*, in *Les Oeuvres libres*, No. 233 (1945), 268.

21. *La Galerie dramatique* (Paris: Éditions Corréa, 1949), p. 101.

22. Letter to the author, dated May 7, 1956.
23. *Ibid.*
24. Jean Renoir, *Orvet* (Paris: Gallimard, 1955), p. 31.
25. *Ibid.*, p. 36.
26. *Ibid.*, p. 56.
27. *Ibid.*, p. 77.
28. *Ibid.*, pp. 183–184.
29. *Ibid.*, pp. 197–198.
30. *Arts*, No. 602, *loc. cit.*

Bibliography

I. The Plays of Pirandello — *In Italian*

The edition of Pirandello's plays used is that of the *Biblioteca Moderna Mondadori*, in 17 volumes, published by Mondadori. These volumes were printed in Verona, but no city of publication is indicated. Dates are listed below for each individual volume.

For an extensive discussion of various editions of Pirandello's works, consult the two volumes of the bibliography prepared by Manlio Lo Vecchio Musti (see p. 163).

1. *La Morsa; Lumìe di Sicilia; Il Dovere del medico.* 1953.
2. *Pensaci, Giacomino! La Regione degli altri.* 1953.
3. *Liolà; Così è (se vi pare).* 1953.
4. *Il Berretto a sonagli; La Giara; Il Piacere dell'onestà.* 1954.
5. *Ma non è una cosa seria; Il Giuoco delle parti.* 1954.
6. *L'Innesto; La Patente; L'Uomo, la bestia e la virtù.* 1955.
7. *Questa sera si recita a soggetto; Trovarsi.* 1951.
8. *Tutto per bene; Come prima, meglio di prima.* 1951.
9. *La Signora Morli una e due; All'uscita; L'Imbecille; Cecè.* 1951.
10. *Vestire gli ignudi; L'Altro figlio; L'Uomo dal fiore in bocca.* 1951.
11. *La Vita che ti diedi; Ciascuno a suo modo.* 1951.
12. *Diana e la Tuda; Sagra del Signore della Nave; Bellavita.* 1951.
13. *L'Amica delle mogli; Non si sa come; Sogno (ma forse no).* 1951.
14. *La Nuova colonia; O di uno o di nessuno.* 1951.

15. *Lazzaro; Come tu mi vuoi.* 1951.
16. *Sei personaggi in cerca d'autore; Enrico IV.* 1954.
17. *Quando si è qualcuno; La Favola del figlio cambiato; I Giganti della montagna.* 1951.

II. THE PLAYS OF PIRANDELLO — *In French*

Between 1950 *and* 1959, *Gallimard, Paris, published the complete theater of Pirandello in French. Except where indicated, the translations are by Benjamin Crémieux. Dates are listed below for each individual volume.*

1. *Six Personnages en quête d'auteur; Chacun Sa Vérité; Henri IV; Comme ci (ou comme ça).* 1950.
2. *Un Imbécile; Comme tu me veux; Diane et Tuda; La Vie que je t'ai donnée.* 1951.
3. *Vêtir ceux qui sont nus; Comme avant, mieux qu'avant; Je rêvais (peut-être)* [Marie-Anne Comnène]; *Cecé* [Comnène]; *La Fleur à la bouche* [Comnène]; *À la Sortie* [Comnène]. 1951.
4. *Tout pour le mieux; Liolà* [Comnène]; *Méfie-toi, Giacomino* [Comnène]; *La Jarre* [Comnène]. 1952.
5. *Ce Soir on improvise; La Fable de l'enfant échangé* [Comnène]; *Les Géants de la montagne* [Comnène]; *L'Autre Fils* [Comnène]. 1953.
6. *La Volupté de l'honneur* [Camille Mallarmé]; *Quand on est quelqu'un* [Louise Servicen]; *L'Homme, la bête et la vertu* [Servicen]. 1954.
7. *Le Bonnet de fou; Se trouver* [Comnène]; *L'Étau* [Comnène]; *Cédrats de Sicilie* [Comnène]; *Bellavita* [Comnène]; *Le Brevet* [Comnène]; *La Raison des autres* [Comnène]; *L'Offrande du Seigneur du navire* [Comnène]. 1956.
8. *Ève et Line; Lazare* [Comnène and Crémieux]; *Ou d'un seul ou d'aucun* [Comnène]; *L'Amie des femmes* [Comnène]; *On ne sait comment* [Comnène]; *C'était pour rire* [Comnène]; *Le Devoir du médecin* [Comnène]. 1957.
9. *La Nouvelle Colonie* [Servicen]; *Le Jeu des rôles* [Servicen]; *La Greffe* [Servicen]. 1959.

III. French Plays Discussed

Achard, Marcel. *Le Corsaire*, in *La Petite Illustration*, No. 872 (May 21, 1938).

———. *Domino*, in *La Petite Illustration*, No. 582 (June 25, 1932).

———. *Jean de la Lune*, in *Histoires d'amour*. Paris: La Table ronde, 1949.

Adam, Alfred. *La Fugue de Caroline*, in *Les Oeuvres libres*, No. 233 (1945), 235–319.

Adamov, Arthur. *Théâtre*, I. (*La Parodie; L'Invasion; La grande et la petite manœuvre; Le Professeur Taranne; Tous contre tous*). Paris: Gallimard, 1953.

Amiel, Denys. *L'Image*, in *Théâtre*, III. Paris: Albin Michel, 1930.

Anouilh, Jean. *Antigone*. Paris: La Table ronde, 1947.

———. *Ardèle ou la Marguerite; La Valse des toréadors; Pauvre Bitos ou le dîner de têtes*, in *Pièces grinçantes*. Paris: La Table ronde, 1956.

———. *Colombe; L'Invitation au château; La Répétition ou l'Amour puni*, in *Pièces brillantes*. Paris: La Table ronde, 1951.

———. *Léocadia; Le Rendez-vous de Senlis*, in *Pièces roses*. Paris: Calmann-Lévy, 1942.

———. *La Sauvage; Le Voyageur sans bagage*, in *Pièces noires*. Paris: Calmann-Lévy, 1942.

———. *Y'avait un prisonnier*, in *La Petite Illustration*, No. 724 (May 18, 1935).

Beckett, Samuel. *En Attendant Godot*. Paris: Éditions de minuit, 1952.

———. *Fin de partie; Acte sans paroles*. Paris: Éditions de minuit, 1957.

Bernard, Jean-Jacques. *Nationale 6*, in *La Petite Illustration*, No. 376 (Nov. 23, 1935).

———. *Le Printemps des autres; L'Invitation au voyage*, in *Théâtre*. Paris: Albin Michel, 1925.

Bernstein, Henry. *La Galerie des glaces*, in *La Petite Illustration*, No. 236 (March 28, 1925).

Camus, Albert. *Le Malentendu; Caligula.* Paris: Gallimard, 1947.

Cocteau, Jean. *Les Chevaliers de la Table Ronde,* in *Théâtre,* I. Paris: Gallimard, 1948.

———. *La Machine infernale.* Paris: Bernard Grasset, 1934.

Crommelynck, Fernand. *Chaud et froid,* in *Les Oeuvres libres,* No. 184 (Oct., 1936), 207–322.

Gantillon, Simon. *Maya.* Paris: Société des spectacles, 1927.

———. *Maya.* New York: The Actor-Managers, Inc., 1928.

Genet, Jean. *Les Bonnes.* Sceaux: Jean-Jacques Pauvert, 1954.

Ghelderode, Michel de. *Trois auteurs, un drame,* in *Théâtre,* II. Paris: Gallimard, 1952.

Ghéon, Henri. *Le Comédien et la Grâce.* Paris: Plon, 1925.

Giraudoux, Jean. *L'Apollon de Bellac.* Paris: Bernard Grasset, 1947.

———. *La Folle de Chaillot.* Paris: Bernard Grasset, 1946.

———. *L'Impromptu de Paris.* Paris: Bernard Grasset, 1937.

———. *Intermezzo.* Paris: Bernard Grasset, 1933.

———. *Siegfried.* Paris: Bernard Grasset, 1928.

Guitry, Sacha. *Quand jouons-nous la comédie!* in *La Petite Illustration,* No. 763 (March 17, 1936).

Ionesco, Eugène. *La Cantatrice chauve,* in *Théâtre.* Paris: Arcanes, 1953.

———. *Les Chaises; Amédée ou Comment s'en débarasser,* in *Théâtre,* I. Paris: Gallimard, 1954.

Lenormand, Henri-René. *Crépuscule du Théâtre,* in *Théâtre complet,* VIII. Paris: Albin Michel, 1935.

———. *L'Homme et ses fantômes.* Paris: G. Crès, 1925.

———. *Mixture,* in *Théâtre complet,* VII. Paris: G. Crès, 1925.

———. *Le Simoun.* Paris: G. Crès, 1921.

———. *Une Vie secrète,* in *Théâtre complet,* III. Paris: G. Crès, 1924.

Libéraki, Marguerite. *L'Autre Alexandre.* Paris: Gallimard, 1957.

Marcel, Gabriel. *La Chapelle ardente,* in *La Petite Illustration,* No. 263 (Nov. 7, 1925).

———. *Le Divertissement posthume,* in *Théâtre comique.* Paris: Albin Michel, 1947.

———. *Un Homme de Dieu,* in *France Illustration théâtrale et littéraire* (Nov. 12, 1949), 1–12.

Neveux, Georges. *Théâtre (Le Voyage de Thésée; Juliette ou la Clé des songes; Ma Chance et ma chanson).* Paris: Juliard, 1946.

——. *Zamore; Plainte contre inconnu.* Paris: La Table ronde, 1953.

Pellerin, Jean-Victor. *Têtes de rechange; Intimité.* Paris: Coutan-Lambert, 1940.

Renoir, Jean. *Orvet.* Paris: Gallimard, 1955.

Romains, Jules. *Donogoo.* Paris: Gallimard, 1950.

——. *Knock.* Paris: Gallimard, 1924.

Salacrou, Armand. *Atlas-Hotel; Les Frénétiques,* in *Théâtre,* II. Paris: Gallimard, 1944.

——. *L'Inconnue d'Arras,* in *Théâtre,* III. Paris: Gallimard, 1942.

——. *La Marguerite; La Terre est ronde,* in *Théâtre,* IV. Paris: Gallimard, 1945.

——. *Les Nuits de la colère,* in *Théâtre,* V. Paris: Gallimard, 1952.

——. *Le Pont de l'Europe,* in *Théâtre,* I. Paris: Gallimard, 1943.

——. *Poof; L'Archipel Lenoir.* Paris: Gallimard, 1950.

Sarment, Jean. *Je suis trop grand pour moi,* in *La Petite Illustration,* No. 4 (1924).

——. *Léopold le bien-aimé,* in *La Petite Illustration,* No. 192 (1927).

——. *Le Pêcheur d'ombres.* Paris: Fasquelle, 1936.

——. *Les plus beaux yeux du monde,* in *La Petite Illustration,* No. 155 (1926).

——. *Sur mon beau navire,* in *La Petite Illustration,* No. 221 (Jan. 5, 1929).

——. *Le Voyage à Biarritz,* in *La Petite Illustration,* No. 400 (Nov. 7, 1936).

Sartre, Jean-Paul. *Le Diable et le Bon Dieu.* Paris: Gallimard, 1951.

——. *Huis clos; Les Mouches, Morts sans sépulture,* in *Théâtre.* Paris: Gallimard, 1947.

——. *Les Mains sales.* Paris: Gallimard, 1948.

——. *Nekrassov.* Paris: Gallimard, 1956.

Savoir, Alfred. *La Couturière de Lunéville*. Paris: Librairie
théâtrale, 1923.
―――. *Le Figurant de la Gaîté*, in *La Fuite en avant*. Paris:
Gallimard, 1930.
Vauthier, Jean. *Le Personnage combattant (fortissimo)*. Paris:
Gallimard, 1955.

IV. CRITICAL AND BIOGRAPHICAL WORKS CONSULTED — *Books*

*For a more extensive bibliography dealing with Pirandello's life
and works, consult Di Pietro's work listed below.*

Alberès, R. M. (pseud. René Marill). *L'Aventure intellectuelle
du XXe siècle*. Paris: La Nouvelle Édition, 1950.
Ambrière, Francis. *La Galerie dramatique*. Paris: Corréa, 1949.
Arnold, Paul, ed. *Théâtre*, III. Paris: Éditions du Pavois, 1945.
Bàccolo, Luigi. *Pirandello*. Milan: Fratelli Bocca, 1949.
Bentley, Eric, ed. *Naked Masks*, by Luigi Pirandello. New York:
E. P. Dutton, 1952.
―――. *The Playwright as Thinker*. New York: Meridian, 1955.
Beraud, Henri. *Retours à pied*. Paris: G. Crès, 1925.
Bontempelli, Massimo. *Pirandello, Leopardi, D'Annunzio*. Verona:
Bompiani, 1939.
Brisson, Pierre. *Au Hasard des soirées*. Paris: Gallimard, 1935.
―――. *Le Théâtre des années folles*. Geneva: Éditions du milieu
du monde, 1943.
Brügger, Maria Künzle. *Le Didascalie nel teatro di Pirandello*.
Lugano: Tell, 1952.
Cantoro, Umberto. *Luigi Pirandello e il problema della personalità*.
Bologna: Nicola Ugo Gallo, 1954.
Clouard, Henri. *Histoire de la littérature française*, II. Paris: Albin
Michel, 1949.
Coindreau, Maurice. *La Farce est jouée*. New York: Éditions de la
Maison Française, 1942.
Crema, Edoardo. *Il Dramma della creazione in Pirandello*. Siena:
Maia, 1953.
Crémieux, Benjamin. *Essai sur l'évolution littéraire de l'Italie, de
1870 à nos jours*. Paris: KRA, 1928.

————. *Henri IV et la dramaturgie de Luigi Pirandello.* Paris: N.R.F., 1928.

————. *Panorama de la littérature italienne contemporaine.* Paris: KRA, 1928.

Daniels, May. *The French Drama of the Unspoken.* Edinburgh: University Press, 1953.

Dickinson, T. H., ed. *The Theatre in Changing Europe.* New York: Holt, 1937.

Didier, Jean. *À la Recherche de Jean Anouilh.* Liège: Les Éditions de la sixaine, 1946.

Doisy, Marcel. *Esquisses.* Paris: André Flament, 1950.

————. *Études.* Paris: André Flament, 1951.

————. *Le Théâtre français contemporain.* Brussels: La Boétie, 1947.

Dumur, Guy. *Pirandello.* Paris: L'Arche, 1955.

Evola, N. D. *Bibliografia degli studi sulla letteratura italiana (1920–1934).* Milan: Vita e pensiero, 1938.

Fazia, Alba-Marie. *Luigi Pirandello and Jean Anouilh.* Unpublished Ph.D. dissertation, Department of French, Columbia University, 1954.

Fergusson, Francis. *The Idea of a Theater.* Garden City: Doubleday Anchor Books, 1954.

Gautier, Jean-Jacques. *Paris sur scène.* Paris: Éditions Jacques Vautrain, 1951.

Gramsci, Antonio. "Il Teatro di Pirandello," in *Letteratura e vita nazionale.* Turin: Einaudi, 1950.

Hobson, Harold. *The French Theatre of Today.* London: George G. Harrap, 1953.

Jouvet, Louis, *Réflexions du comédien.* Paris: Librairie théâtrale, 1952.

Knowles, Dorothy. *La Réaction idéaliste au théâtre depuis 1890.* Paris: Droz, 1934.

Lalou, René. *Le Théâtre en France depuis 1900.* Paris: Presses universitaires de France, 1951.

Lamm, Martin. *Modern Drama.* New York: Philosophical Library, 1953.

Landers, W., ed. *Antigone,* by Jean Anouilh. London: George G. Harrap, 1954.

Lauretta, Enzo. *Pirandello umano e irreligioso*. Milan: Castaldi, 1954.

Lenormand, Henri-René. *Les Confessions d'un auteur dramatique*. 2 vols. Paris: Albin Michel, 1949–1953.

————. *Les Pitoëff*. Paris: Odette Lieutier, 1943.

Lo Vecchio Musti, Manlio. *Bibliografia di Pirandello*, 2 vols. Milan: Mondadori, 1937–1940.

————. *L'Opera di Luigi Pirandello*. Turin: Paravia, 1939.

MacClintock, Lander. *The Age of Pirandello*. Bloomington: Indiana University Press, 1951.

Marsh, Edwin Owen. *Jean Anouilh, Poet of Pierrot and Pantaloon*. London: W. H. Allen, 1953.

Mortier, Alfred. *Quinze Ans de théâtre*. Paris: Albert Messein, 1933.

Nardelli, Federico Vittore. *L'Uomo segreto*. Milan: Mondadori, 1944.

Palmer, John. *Studies in Contemporary Theatre*. London: Martin Secker, 1927.

Paolantonacci, J.–Th. *Le Théâtre de Luigi Pirandello*. Paris: Nouvelles Editions latines, n. d.

Pietro, Antonio di. *Pirandello*. Milan: Vita e pensiero, 1951.

Pitoëff, Georges. *Notre Théâtre*. Paris: Messages, 1949.

Praga, Marco. *Cronache teatrali, 1923*. Milan: Treves, 1924.

Radine, Serge. *Anouilh, Lenormand, Salacrou, trois dramaturges à la recherche de leur vérité*. Geneva: Édition des trois collines, 1951.

————. *Essais sur le théâtre*. Geneva: Les Éditions du Mont-Blanc, 1944.

Rageot, Gaston. *Prise de vues*. Paris: La Nouvelle Revue critique, 1928.

Raymond, Marcel. *Le Jeu retrouvé*. Montréal: Éditions de l'Arbre, 1943.

Rhodes, S. A. *The Contemporary French Theatre*. New York: Crofts, 1942.

————. "France and Belgium," in *A History of Modern Drama*, ed. Barrett Clark and George Freedly. New York: Appleton-Century, 1947.

Sée, Edmond. *Le Mouvement dramatique*. Paris: Éditions de France, 1930.

———. *Le Théâtre français contemporain*. Paris: A. Cohn, 1950.

Sion, Georges. *Le Théâtre français de l'entre-deux guerres*. Paris: Castermann, n. d.

Starkie, Walter. *Luigi Pirandello*. London: J. M. Dent, 1926. 2d ed., New York: E. P. Dutton, 1937.

Tilgher, Adriano. *Studi sul teatro contemporaneo*. Rome: Libreria di scienze e lettere, 1928.

Touchard, Pierre-Aimé. *Dionysos*. Paris: Éditions du seuil, 1949.

Vittorini, Domenico. *The Drama of Luigi Pirandello*. Philadelphia: University of Pennsylvania Press, 1935.

Werrie, Paul. *Le Théâtre de la fuite*. Brussels-Paris: Les Écrits, 1943.

Williams, Raymond. *Drama from Ibsen to Eliot*. London: Chatto and Windus, 1952.

Zoja, Nella. *Pirandello*. Brescia: Morcelliana, 1954.

V. CRITICAL AND BIOGRAPHICAL WORKS CONSULTED — *Articles*

"À Paris et ailleurs," *Les Nouvelles Littéraires*, No. 1286 (April 24, 1952), 7.

Alley, J. N. "French Periodical Criticism of Pirandello's Plays," *Italica*, XXV (June, 1948), 138–149.

Amico, Silvio d'. "Fortuna di Pirandello, 1936–1952," *Rivista di studi teatrali*, I, No. 3–4 (July–Dec., 1952), 248–269.

Anouilh, Jean. "Godot ou le sketch des Pensées de Pascal traité par les Fratellini," *Arts*, No. 400 (Feb. 27–March 5, 1953), 1.

Bàccolo, Luigi. "Pirandello, uomo 'che non sapeva nulla,'" *Sipario*, No. 55 (Nov., 1950).

Bernard, Marc. "Le Théâtre: *Six Personnages en quête d'auteur*," *Les Nouvelles Littéraires*, No. 1280 (March 13, 1952), 8.

Bertolini, Alberto. "Pirandelliana," *Ridotto*, No. 1 (1951), 12–14.

Billy, André. "Revue de la quinzaine: Théâtre," *Mercure de France*, CLXXVIII (March 15, 1925), 762–765.

Brée, Germaine. "Georges Neveux: A Theatre of Adventure," *Yale French Studies*, XIV (Winter, 1954–1955), 65–70.

Chastaing, Maxime. "L'Uomo come protagonista nel teatro francese contemporaneo," *Rivista di studi teatrali*, I, No. 1 (Jan.–March, 1952), 44–57.

"Copeau a renové le théâtre," *Arts* (Oct. 29–Nov. 4, 1952), 1, 10.

Crémieux, Benjamin. "Luigi Pirandello," *Revue de Paris*, XLI, No. 23 (Dec. 1, 1934), 686–700.

———. "Les Tendances actuelles du théâtre," *Encyclopédie française*, XVII, December, 1935, Chap. ii, "Les Arts du temps," iv, 1–12.

———. "Le Théâtre: *Six Personnages en quête d'auteur*," *La Nouvelle Revue française*, XX (June 1, 1923), 960–966.

Croce, Benedetto. "Luigi Pirandello," XXIII, *La Critica* (1935), 20–33.

Fiocco, Achille. "The Heritage of Pirandello," *World Theatre*, III, No. 3, 24–30.

Janner, Arminio. "Luigi Pirandello e la letteratura contemporanea," *Nuova Antologia*, Dec., 1946, pp. 313–327.

Jeanson, Francis. "Pirandello et Camus à travers Henri IV et Caligula," *Les Temps modernes*, No. 61 (Nov., 1950), 944–953.

Lemarchand, Jacques. "*Six personnages* de Luigi Pirandello à la Comédie Française," *Le Figaro littéraire*, No. 308 (March 15, 1952), 10.

Lo Vecchio Musti, Manlio. "La Diffusione dell'opera pirandelliana all'estero," *Romana*, III, Nos. 5–6 (May–June, 1939), 355–364.

Lynes, Carlos, Jr. "Adamov or 'le sens littéral' in the Theatre," *Yale French Studies*, XIV (Winter, 1954–1955), 48–56.

Mallarmé, Camille. "Comment Luigi Pirandello fut révélé au public parisien le 20 décembre, 1922," *Revue de l'histoire du théâtre*, I (1955), 7–37.

May, Frederick. "Drama of Reality," *Drama* (Winter, 1954), 21–26.

Nathan, Monique. "Pirandello et le pirandellisme," *Monde-Nouveau-Paru*, No. 49, 48–53.

Oulmont, Ch. "Le Vrai Visage de Pirandello," *Revue Théâtrale*, Nos. 9–10 (1949), 19–24.

"Pirandello vous a-t-il influencé?" *Arts*, No. 602 (Jan. 16–22, 1957), 2.

Rageot, Gaston. "Le Pirandellisme," *Revue politique et littéraire*, LXIV, No. 12 (June 19, 1926), 383–385.

Reboul, Fernand. "De Pirandello au pirandellisme," *Études italiennes*, I (April–June, 1931), 80–97.

Renaud, Luc. "Le Théâtre italien en France," *Paris-Théâtre*, No. 75 (Aug., 1953), 6–10.

Ridenti, Lucio. "L'Héritage de Pirandello," *La Revue théâtrale*, VII (1948), 16–18.

Ruff, Marcel. "Corneille et Pirandello," *Cahiers du Sud*, No. 299 (1st semester, 1950), 109–114.

Sciascia, L. "Pirandello et le pirandellisme," *Revue des lettres modernes*, No. 4 (May, 1954), 1–16; Nos. 5–6 (June–July, 1954), 17–45.

Théâtre de France, No. 3 (1953), 125.

Vowles, Richard, B. "Existentialism and Dramatic Form," *Educational Theatre Journal* (Oct., 1953), 215–219.

Wandruszka, Mario. "Luigi Pirandello," *Deutsche Vierteljahrsschrift*, No. 2 (1954), 234–247.

Worms-Barretta, Rose. "Le Théâtre de Pirandello," *La Revue hebdomadaire*, XLIV, No. 5 (Feb. 2, 1935), 18–41.

VI. Personal Letters by French Playwrights

The following letters, sent by French playwrights to the author of this study, are referred to in this book:

by Marcel Achard, dated March 2, 1956;
by Denys Amiel, dated March 13, 1956;
by Jean-Jacques Bernard, dated March 19, 1956;
by Jean Cocteau, dated March 10, 1956;
by Gabriel Marcel, dated March 12, 1956;
by Jean Renoir, dated May 7, 1956;
by Jules Romains, dated March 15, 1956;
by Armand Salacrou, dated February 8, 1957.

Index

The main treatment of any particular entry is referred to in italics.

PIRANDELLO
and the French Theater

THOMAS BISHOP
With a Foreword by Germaine Brée

Early in the 1920's a play by an Italian author unknown in France was presented on the Paris stage. Overnight the playwright, Luigi Pirandello, conquered Parisian theatergoers and excited the creative imagination of French directors and writers. Pirandello's influence was to be the shaping factor throughout the next two decades and has again been prominent in the postwar works of Sartre, Beckett, Ionesco, and others.

The subject matter of most of Pirandello's plays is in the realm of ideas—complex ideas concerning reality and illusion, the human personality, and the basic problem of artistic creation. Some of the French playwrights—Romains, Jean-Jacques Bernard, Sarment—were giving dramatic form to similar ideas when Pirandello was first introduced to France, but the full impact of his themes and techniques struck the young writers—Anouilh, Salacrou, Giraudoux, and Neveux. Still others have been indirectly influenced, their works reflecting the essence of Pirandello as his plays have become a "fixture" of the Paris theater over the past four decades.